SPIRITUAL RESILIENCE
85 Lessons for Teens Navigating Difficult Times

SPIRITUAL RESILIENCE

85 Lessons for Teens Navigating Difficult Times

By Eliud A. Montoya

STUDENT'S NAME:

_____

PALABRA PURA
palabra-pura.com
2024

> I dedicate this book to Eva Maria and David Eliud, my children

Spiritual Resilience: 85 Lessons for Teens Navigating Difficult Times
Copyright © 2024 by Eliud A. Montoya

ISBN: 978-1-951372-53-8
Paperback

NIV: Scripture quotations marked (NIV) are taken from the Holy Bible, New International Version®, NIV®. Copyright © 1973, 1978, 1984, 2011 by Biblica, Inc.™ Used by permission of Zondervan. All rights reserved worldwide. www.zondervan.com The "NIV" and "New International Version" are trademarks registered in the United States Patent and Trademark Office by Biblica, Inc.

KJV: Scripture quotations from The Authorized (King James) Version. Rights in the Authorized Version in the United Kingdom are vested in the Crown. Reproduced by permission of the Crown's patentee, Cambridge University Press

NLT: Scripture quotations marked (NLT) are taken from the Holy Bible, New Living Translation, copyright ©1996, 2004, 2015 by Tyndale House Foundation. Used by permission of Tyndale House Publishers, a Division of Tyndale House Ministries, Carol Stream, Illinois 60188. All rights reserved.

ESV: Scripture quotations marked (ESV) are taken from the ESV® Bible (The Holy Bible, English Standard Version®), copyright © 2001 by Crossway, a publishing ministry of Good News Publishers. Used by permission. All rights reserved.

All rights reserved. No part of this publication may be reproduced, distributed, or transmitted in any form or by any means, including photocopying, recording, or other electronic or mechanical methods, without the prior written permission of the publisher, except as permitted by U.S. copyright law.

To request permission, contact palabrapura@outlook.com
We greatly appreciate HONORING the copyright of this document and do not retransmit or make copies of it in any form (except for strictly personal use). Thank you for your respectful cooperation.

Book's design: Palabra Pura
www.palabra-pura.com

RELIGION/ Christian Education/Teens
Printed in the United States of America

Table of Contents

Foreword **XI**

PART I. KNOWING GOD THROUGH HIS SON 1

    1. The Creator of all **1**

    2. God wants to be your friend **3**

    3. God is love **5**

    4. The Great Tragedy **7**

    5. The Great Solution to the Great Tragedy **9**

    6. How to Become a Child of God **11**

PART II. DOCTRINE 15

    7. If Jesus Dwells in your Heart, you will Speak of Him **15**

    8. Seeing the Face of Jesus Every Day **17**

    9. Jesus Rose Again on The Third Day **19**

    10. The Bible is the Truth **21**

    11. Jesus Continues to Heal the Sick **23**

    12. Jesus Baptizes in the Holy Spirit **25**

    13. John Baptizes Jesus in the Jordan **27**

    14. Christ is Coming Soon **29**

    15. Dinning with Jesus **31**

PART III. THE MORAL LAW OF GOD 33

    16. Worship God Alone **33**

    17. Religious Images **35**

    18. The Name of God is Sacred **37**

    19. The Day of Rest **39**

    20. Honor Thy Father and Thy Mother **41**

    21. Thou Shalt Not Kill **43**

PART III. THE MORAL LAW OF GOD (continued)

    22. Abortion **45**

    23. Do not Harm your Body **47**

    24. Fidelity in Marriage **49**

    25. You Must Respect the Property of Others **51**

    26. Always Tell the Truth **53**

    27. Be Happy with What You Have Now **55**

PART IV. CHRISTIAN CHARACTER **57**

    28. Judge not Lest you Be Judged **57**

    29. We are the Salt of the Earth and the Light of the World **59**

    30. See No One Unclothed **61**

    31. Fasting **63**

    32. True Wealth **65**

    33. Help the Poor **67**

    34. Do Not Be Angry **69**

    35. Missionaries **71**

    36. Be Grateful **73**

    37. Fear of God **75**

    38. Keep your Faith and Trust in Jesus **77**

    39. Watch your Thoughts **79**

    40. The Great Commission **81**

    41. Main Types of Prayer **83**

    42. Use AI Responsibly **85**

PART V. LEADERSHIP FOUNDATIONS **87**

    43. Racial Discrimination **87**

    44. The Great Value of Work **89**

    45. Giving for God **91**

    46. Saving Money **93**

    47. Spending Money **95**

PART V. LEADERSHIP FOUNDATIONS (continued)

48. Seek to Serve, Not to Be Served **97**

49. Keep your Promises **99**

50. Obey your Authorities **101**

51. Discipline **103**

52. Your Talents **105**

53. Learn to Plan **107**

54. Learn to Say NO! **109**

55. Be a Good Leader **111**

56. Video Games **113**

PART VI. RELATIONSHIPS WITH OTHERS **115**

57. The Design of Family **115**

58. Respect for the Elderly **117**

59. Babies are a Blessing **119**

60. Adoption **121**

61. Our Friends **123**

62. Compassion for Others **125**

63. Grandparents **127**

64. The Power of Your Tongue **129**

65. How to Distinguish a True Christian **131**

66. Do not Compare Yourself with Others **135**

67. Forgive Always **137**

68. If you Make a Mistake, Ask for Forgiveness at Once **139**

69. Accept People as They Are **141**

70. Use of Social Media **143**

PART VII. YOUR IDENTITY **145**

71. Your Sex is your Sex **145**

72. Beware of Manipulators **147**

73. Suffering is Normal **149**

74. Be Generous **151**

75. Be Humble **153**

76. Stay Away from Temptation **155**

77. Taking Important Decisions **157**

78. Don't Live by Emotions **159**

79. The Meaning of "Good Life" **161**

80. God is Always Good **163**

81. Control your Feelings **165**

82. Be a True Man **167**

83. Be a True Woman **169**

84. Levels of Intimacy **173**

85. Do Not Accept False Ideas **177**

Foreword

I have titled this book *Spiritual Resilience: 85 Lessons for Teens Navigating Difficult* Times. Why? Because there are a multitude of fierce and terrible attacks on Christians like you; diabolical attacks that will try to turn you away from faith in Christ. But you must be smart and wise, and show resilience, that is, you must withstand all the storms and stand firm in the Lord Jesus.

I have written it, first of all, for my own children, who at this precise moment are going through that age, but also for hundreds of thousands of other boys and girls who are at that stage as well.

This book is designed for teaching boys and girls your age, and it will teach you the surest ways to live a powerful life. It is a journey, and on this journey, you must cooperate willingly; submitting to the guidance of the Holy Spirit, trusting that God is wiser than all the human beings in the world, including those who devised the super technology that exists today. So, with this book, we will be fellow travelers. Will you join us?

Seven parts

The book is divided into seven parts, each of which is vital. The first shows you the way to meet Jesus Christ. It shows you that all human beings need a Savior, and this Savior is called Jesus Christ. But not only does He save you, He requires you to make Him your Lord as well, which means that if you really want to spend eternity with Him, you need to obey what He says. In the Bible we have what God says, and what the Lord expects of us.

The second part talks about Christian doctrine. This section contains the most important elements of Christian doctrine that will help you to have a structure of faith. Your mind was designed to have structures in all areas of life, so also your faith needs to have a structure: God, in His Word, has given us these doctrines, and each one of them is indispensable to build a firm foundation for your faith.

Next. we will look at part III entitled "The Moral Law of God". This section is very important, because it consists of the explanation of what God has willed to be good and what is evil. The moral life does not depend on the thought of each one, nor on how each one understands it, but God has already told us what is good and what is evil. If you or any person does not understand this section well, then he will tend to perversion. The perversion consists in calling good evil and good evil. That is why this section is very fundamental.

In Part IV we will look at Christian character. In other words, what is the behavior and way of thinking of a Christian. Christians think in a particular way and form a character, which we call *Christian character*. It is very important that you base your behavior and your words on the Scriptures; and in this part we will look at some of the most essential issues.

Part V consists of the basics of leadership. All Christians are leaders in one way or another, and in this section, you will learn how to be one. Whoever is not a leader in the church, nor is the secular world, is a leader without him or her realizing it. Everyone is watching us, and our behavior will have an impact on at least one person in life, but perhaps many more. You must learn this part very well too.

Part VI deals with issues related to social relationships, that is, with other people. These people start with your own family; if you do not know how to live with the members of your own family you will hardly be able to build lasting relationships. This part is essential for your personal happiness and success, and for the good (through yourself) of those you meet in life.

Finally, in Part VII, you will learn about your identity. Although we are all different in many ways, there are also things that we have common identities or that many people share. This part is very important for you to be able to satisfy very important areas in your life, and for your life to have a clear meaning. A person who lacks identity, or who does not understand his identity well, will be an easy prey of the devil and will end up falling into his nets.

How to Use this Book

Each lesson in this book has a repetitive structure, and is designed for learning. A key Bible verse has been chosen for you to memorize. This verse contains the most important truth of the topic being covered. Remember that rather than relying on any human philosophy's book or personal thoughts, the basis of our faith and conduct is the Bible, that is why the Scriptures must be memorized so that they are within your heart. After that, the first paragraph is a paragraph that introduces in a general way the topic that will be discussed, so you should pay close attention to this paragraph.

The instructor (your dad, mom, teacher or professor) who is giving you the class will always be available to help you with anything you don't understand, so don't hesitate to ask him/her any questions you may have. Together with you, they will read the material, but they will explain and clarify to you what they want to emphasize.

You will notice that there are a few questions. These are questions that will help you develop your critical thinking. Critical thinking is very important in getting to the truth in any matter. All well-educated people have been trained in this type of thinking, and this book will help you a lot in it. Do your best to answer them, no evaluation of your answers is necessary, and usually, the answers will vary from person to person, so don't worry at all; just relax and answer freely.

There are then two sections. The first is called "Bible Story" and the second "Illustration". In the first one I make a preliminary explanation of concepts and ideas that need to be well established, and then I comment on the biblical passage that contains a story on the subject. It is necessary, of course, that you are not satisfied with just the brief explanation that I make of this story, but that you must read it for yourself in the Bible. Ideally, you should read this story in class. Afterward, in the "Illustration" section, I include a story (often from the secular world) that is related to the topic, by the way, almost always this story is based on real life.

What follows is a series of questions that you should answer to the best of your ability. The answers to these questions are there, in the sections you have read with your instructor or yourself. Try to answer them from memory, without having to go back over what you have read. However, if you need to review the information do it, what really matters is that you do not, for any reason, fail to answer these questions.

Then you will see a list of sentences or phrases to memorize. These are the key concepts of the lesson, the ideas that must be anchored in your mind and heart in order to complete the learning process. Finally, there is also a list of other Bible verses that are related to the topic, and that will be very good for you to look them up and take the time to memorize them as well.

There are some lessons that are atypical, that is, they are different from the others. These lessons will help you to take your mind off the routine, on the one hand, and on the other hand, they are topics that require additional information. You will find that these lessons are very interesting, and require further explanation and discussion.

This book is a journey we will travel together. A journey of possibly two years. You are growing, and you need to have this knowledge to face the challenges and storms of life that will try to divert you from faith in Jesus Christ. That is why I have titled this book *Spiritual Resilience*.

Eliud A. Montoya

Oklahoma, 2024.

Part I. Knowing God Through His Son

1

The Creator of All

Memorize

Genesis 1:1 "In the beginning God created the heaven and the earth".

Everything that exists on earth must have a Creator. When you see a building, you certainly don't think it was made by itself. When you see a bicycle, you can surely imagine that there was someone who thought about how to make it, that is, designed it, made the parts, and finally assembled it. In the same way, everything in nature (including all the animals and yourself) was created by God. God created all that, many, many years ago. No one knows how long ago everything was created, but what we can know is that God created it.

❓ Introductory Questions

> 1. Why do you think God wanted to create human beings?
> 2. How is the human being different from everything else in creation (different from animals, for example)?
> 3. Do you think God loves His creation? Why do you think He loves it?

Bible Story (Genesis 1:1-30; 2:7, 18, 21-24)

We do not know how God created the universe. God created the planets, and things we've never known, and may never know. One day, God wanted to make our planet, planet Earth. The Bible says that the planet Earth was dark and that it was in disorder. Then God said, "Let there be light; and there was light." He created a time for there to be light, and he called that period day; also, the period where there is no light but darkness, he called night. That is what God created on the first day.

Then, on the second day, God created the sky and everything in it, although he had not yet created the birds. On the third day God separated the waters from the dry land (the seas and the continents), He also created all vegetation. On the fourth day, God created the sun, the moon and the stars. On the fifth day God created all the living creatures in the seas and also all the birds. On the sixth day, God created the animals; but also, on the sixth day, God created the most special being of all: man. Why is man more special than everything else God created? Because God wanted him to be like Him, to have thoughts, emotions, and to be able to make decisions; also, just as God is spirit, man has a spirit. On what day did God create man? Yes, that's right, on the sixth day! Do you want to know how God created man? He took dust from the earth and then blew on it. Do you know how He created woman? God made Adam to sleep and took a rib from him, and from the rib He created woman.

Illustration

Isaac Newton (the famous inventor) had an atheist friend (an atheist is a person who does not believe that God exists). Isaac's friend believed that the universe was created itself, "it made itself", he said. One day Isaac did a project for school; he made a model of the solar system, all the planets were the perfect size, and the distances between them too; everything was in its place. It was a very extraordinary job! When Isaac took the project he had done to school and his friend saw it, he exclaimed, "Isaac, that model of the solar system is magnificent! Who made it?" Then Isaac replied to his friend, "No one made it, it made itself."

❓ Questions About the Class

1. What did God create on the first day?
2. How did God create man?
3. How did God create woman?
4. Why are man and woman a special creation?
5. What did Isaac's friend say?
6. What did Isaac say when his friend asked him who made the model of the solar system?

Phrases to Memorize

1. God's creation is very complicated and human beings understand very little about it.
2. God is the only being that has not been created, He is the Creator.
3. God created everything that exists in six days.
4. God first created man and then created woman.

The human being is very different from animals, because he resembles God.

Other Bible passages on the theme for reading and memorization

Ps. 139: 13-14; Rom. 1:20; Col. 1:16; Jer. 32:17; Ps. 121:1-2; Is. 40:28.

2

God wants to be your friend

Memorize

Exodus 33:11 "Thus the Lord used to speak to Moses face to face, as a man speaks to his friend".

God created everything that exists, but He created man special, because He created him similar to Himself in several aspects, in what way is man similar to God? Well, God, from the beginning, wanted to have communion with the man and woman He had created. Every day, God visited Adam and Eve to talk with them. Our God is a personal God, who desires not only to be with us, but in us.

? Introductory Questions

1. How do you feel when you have an important friend?
2. Did you know that God – being the most powerful and important Being in the universe – is good to everyone and wants to be everyone's friend?
3. What does it mean to you to be a best friend? Do you like having friends? Do you want God to be your friend and you to be God's friend?

Bible Story (Genesis 18:1-17)

In the Book of Genesis, we begin to understand what God is like and how He treats man and woman. In the beginning, God talked to Adam and Eve; then the Bible tells us that there was a man who walked with God, his name was Enoch. Then again, we see God talking to a man named Noah. It seems that the stories of Genesis are about people who were close to God and often talked with Him. If a person continues reading the Bible, he will realize that God likes to talk to human beings, and the more the better.

In the Book of Genesis, we can read the story of a very special man named Abraham. Abraham is special because in the Bible he is called God's friend. He is called so because God told Abraham about his plans. One day, God went to visit Abraham in the evening, and Abraham saw that He was coming with angels. You should know that God is spirit and cannot be seen, but sometimes He has appeared in visible form in the stories of the Old Testament (the Old Testament is the first part of the Bible). Well, that time, God visited Abraham, told him that his wife and he were going to have a son the following year, and also told him that He had plans to destroy some cities where there were very bad people, these cities were called Sodom and Gomorrah. On that occasion, Abraham tried to convince God not to do it. Could he convince him? No! Because there was no good person in that place except Lot (Abraham's nephew), and God sent his angels to rescue him. One of the great lessons of this story is that God is a personal God, for he told Abraham his plans.

Illustration

Many years ago, there was a very powerful king who had many servants. This king lived with his wife (the queen), and he had a son. Although there were many servants in the palace, this boy's mother liked to visit her son before bedtime, say a prayer with him and cover him with a sheet or blanket. She would always ask him, "Son, are you warm enough? Also, his father, the king, liked to ride with his son on horseback. They would ride together through the meadows and talk. Both the king and the queen had many servants who could do this, but the prince did not like anyone else to do it, he wanted dad and mom to be near him so they could talk.

Questions About the Class

1. Can you remember some of the people God talked to in the Book of Genesis?
2. What was the name of a man who walked with God?
3. Why is Abraham a special person in the Bible?
4. Why do you think God wanted to come personally to talk to Abraham and not just send his angels?
5. Why did the boy in the illustration like to be served by his mother?
6. Why did the boy in the illustration like to ride horses with his dad?

Phrases to Memorize

1. God is a personal God, and He created us to have communion with Him.
2. God wants to be my friend.
3. He expects me to want to be His friend too, because He does not force anyone to be His friend.
4. The way I can be a friend of God is to be a friend of His Son Jesus.

Other Bible passages on the theme for reading and memorization

Jer. 31:3; Jn. 3:16; Gal. 2:20; Eph. 5:2, 25; Jn. 15:15; Tit. 3:4; 1 Jn. 3:1.

3

God is Love

Memorize

1 Jn. 4:8 "Anyone who does not love does not know God, because God is love."

I want to tell you a little more about God. God is not only the most powerful Being in existence, but He is also a God who loves all of His creation, but especially loves human beings. He wants to be friends with all the men and women of the world (including boys and girls, and young men and women like you). Whether you love Him or not, God loves you. Whether you do the right thing or not, He loves you. The greatest demonstration of God's love is that He sent His Son Jesus Christ to die on the cross for you and for everyone, and He did this even for the most evil people in the world.

❓ Questions About the Class

1. What would you do if you knew that another boy/girl was speaking badly about you in front of others?
2. Can you love and treat well those who treat you badly?
3. How do you imagine God's love? How do you feel when someone loves you? Do you want to open your heart to receive God's love?

Bible Story (Genesis 18:1-17)

It is true that God loves everyone, even the most wicked; but not everyone opens their heart to God. The Bible tells us that satan (God's archenemy) deceives human beings to make them believe that God does not love them. That is what this enemy of us and of God taught Eve (the first woman) in the Garden of Eden and unfortunately, she believed him. Since then, many more have been deceived.

Jesus is the Son of God. Jesus came into the world to fulfill a mission; do you know what this mission was? He became man being God (without ceasing to be God) to die as a man on the Cross, do you know this story of love? Well, many times Jesus showed us God's love for everyone, even for the most evil ones. Jesus had many followers, but He chose twelve to be with Him and to be His friends. One of these friends of Jesus was Judas. Judas was a very good man and was a good friend of Jesus, but satan tricked him into believing that Jesus did not really love him. So, he went to Jesus' enemies and told them that if they gave him money, he would deliver Jesus to them to be crucified.

The night Jesus was arrested, He had dinner with His disciples, His twelve friends, and you know what? Jesus knew that Judas had betrayed Him. But He didn't show him hatred or contempt, but love. He let him eat from his plate, washed his feet and called him "friend". Jesus' love is unconditional.

Illustration

A happy family of father, mother and son lived in New York when many were immigrating to California (1844-1855) because they said there was gold there. The father was encouraged to go, and temporarily left his family until he could earn enough money to bring her to live with him. The mother waited patiently. Until one day, she was overjoyed to learn that her husband had sent her the money so they could travel. So they boarded a boat from New York to San Francisco. As they were traveling on the ship, someone started shouting, "Fire, fire!". The captain then realized two things: that it was impossible to put out the fire because it had advanced too far, and that the ship would explode because it was carrying a cargo of gunpowder. So they resorted to the lifeboats; however, there was not enough room. After getting as many people on board as they could, there was only room for one more person, and the mother and son were still on the ship. A decision had to be made. Then the mother kissed her son and said, "Son, you go, and tell your daddy that I died in your place."

❓ Questions About the Class

1. Who does God love, only the good ones?
2. How does satan deceive people? What does he make them believe?
3. Why is the story of Jesus' death on the cross a love story?
4. Why did Judas betray Jesus? How did Jesus show Judas that he loved him, even though he had betrayed Him?
5. Why did the mother in the story decide to die instead of her son?
6. How is the story in the illustration similar to the love story of Jesus?

Phrases to Memorize

1. God loves everyone. He loves us, even if we do not love Him and offend Him.
2. God offers us His love through Jesus, who died for each one of us.
3. Just as God loves everyone (even His enemies), His children, those who open their hearts to receive His love, also love their enemies.
4. The Father's greatest demonstration of love was to send his Son Jesus to die in our place.

Other Bible passages on the theme for reading and memorization

Tit. 3:4; Jn. 3:16; 1 Jn. 4:8-10; 2 Ts. 2.10; Rom. 5:8; Rom 9:1-3; Mt. 5:44; 2 Cor. 5:14-15; 1 Ti. 2:15; Mk. 10:20-22; Mt. 26:50; Jn. 5:34; Lk. 23:34; Rom. 11:28; Jer. 31:3.

4
The Great Tragedy

Memorize

Romans 3:23 "For all have sinned and fall short of the glory of God".

Although God wants to be man's friend and loves us, He cannot have communion with man, because man is evil and He is good. You see, God created man good, but sin made him evil. It all began in the Garden of Eden. God wanted man to be His friend forever, but something tragic happened in the Garden of Eden and for this reason, God could no longer converse with man as before. Man alone chose to be separated from God. Sin always separates us from God. Do you know what sin means? Sin means to do or not to do what God says to do or not to do.

? Introductory Questions

1. Do you think there are bad people in the world? Why?
2. If God is good to everyone, why do you think God doesn't like sin?
3. Why is sin bad for you?

Bible Story (Genesis 3:1-17)

God created man and woman perfect, and He desired that they would live forever with Him. They lived in a beautiful garden called Eden. There they had everything and were very happy. But you know what, the greatest happiness of human beings wasn't living in that beautiful place, but that they lived in obedience to God. If you obey God, you will be happy.

So it was that God told them not to eat the fruit of a tree called "the tree of the knowledge of good and evil"; and He also told them that if they ate of that tree they would die. One day satan, the enemy of God, appeared to Eve and told her that God had lied to them; that God did not want them to be as important as He was, and that is why He forbade them to eat from the tree. Then he told them that they could be gods. Do you think that a creation can become God? No! It is impossible, no one c be God because only God is the Creator. But you know what? Adam and Eve fell into the trap, and they disobeyed God. What happened was exactly what God said: they died because every person who has no friendship with God is dead to Him. Sin causes a person to be separated from God, and when he is separated from God, even if he breathes, he is dead inside.

Illustration

Do you remember who an atheist is? Exactly! A person who doesn't believe in God. Well, a pastor went to a barber to have his beard trimmed. But that barber was an atheist, and as they were talking, the atheist said to the pastor, "If God exists, why are there so many bad people in the world?" At that moment, they both saw a man with a big, long beard passing by on the street. Then the pastor said to the atheist barber, "There is no such thing as a barber!" "Why?" —said the barber. "Because look, there's the proof, that man has a big beard, therefore, barbers don't exist". Then the barber understood that the reason why there were bad people in the world was not because God did not exist, but because they did not approach God, just as men who have a big beard do not go to the barber to have them cut and trimmed.

❓ Questions About the Class

1. What is the greatest happiness of men and women?
2. What did God tell them would happen to Adam and Eve if they disobeyed him?
3. What was the lie that satan told Eve to convince her to disobey God?
4. What does sin cause? What happens if a person separates himself from God?
5. What was the question that the barber asked the pastor?
6. What did the barber understand at the end of the story?

Phrases to Memorize

1. Sin separates me from God, and to be separated from God means to be dead.
2. Every person who does wrong is separated from God.
3. Satan will always tell me that sinning is not "so bad," but he is a liar, because sin causes death.
4. The solution to freedom from sin is to ask God for forgiveness from the heart and to believe in His Son Jesus Christ as Savior and Lord.

Other Bible passages on the theme for reading and memorization

Ez. 18:4; Rom. 6:23; Gal. 5:19-21; 1 Jn. 8-10; Is. 59:2; Jn. 8:34; Rom. 6:16; 5:12; Jas. 1:15.

5

The Great Solution to the Great Tragedy

Memorize

Romans 6:23 "For he wages of sin is dead, but the gift of God is eternal life in Christ Jesus our Lord.

Wages: payment.

Friendship with God is broken because of human sin. It was as if the earth opened up when man and woman sinned, and they were separated from God by a great chasm. Man needed God, but he could not approach Him because He is holy. God continued to love man, but now there was a serious problem in their relationship. How could this be solved? There was a price to pay and no one but God Himself could pay it. The problem was this: God is the offended one, but He is also the judge. Because He is a God of love, God forgives us, but because He is the judge, He could not acquit the guilty.

❓ Introductory Questions

> 1. If a person kills another person, should they go to jail? Yes/no, why?
> 2. Do you know who Jesus is?
> 3. How would you describe Jesus?

Bible Story (Luke 23:26-56)

Jesus is the only-begotten Son of God. This means that God has a Son, but that Son is like Him, that is, Jesus is also God. Jesus and God (the Father) are God, but they are one God. No one understands this because no human being can understand God, but God is like this: God is one, but there are three persons, the Father, the Son and the Holy Spirit.

The only way God could restore His communion with man was for Himself to pay the price for our sins. You see, when mankind sinned before God, He needed to be judged for his crimes, and there was no way that mankind could be innocent before God, he was guilty and needed to pay for it. For example, if a person breaks the law, for example, kills another, he needs to pay for what he did. The condemnation for sin is hell, a place under the earth where there is fire. God then sent his Son into the world. He was born of the virgin Mary and lived among us. Then He was killed on a cross, He was crucified. Why was He crucified? To pay the debt we needed to pay and could not, none of our good works could pay our debt to God and be with him again. Jesus died for you and me so that we could have peace with God and be with Him for eternity. Why did Jesus do that? Because He loved us so much. God loves you and wants you to be His friend forever.

Illustration

There was a just judge who always did what was right. Everyone respected the authority of that judge because he did everything according to the law. One day his mother committed a crime and she appeared before him to be judged. He loved his mother dearly, but he could not simply forgive her because that would be an act of corruption, that is, something bad. Therefore, he got down from the judge's chair and said, "I am going to pay for my mother's crimes." With this, this judge was demonstrating that he was a just judge, but at the same time, he was showing that he loved his mother very much. Thus, Jesus, being in heaven, and being the judge of all, came to earth to die on the cross and pay for the crimes (for the sin) that we had committed.

Questions About the Class

1. Who is Jesus?
2. God is one, but He is revealed in three persons. Who are these three persons?
3. Who was the only person who could pay for our sins?
4. What is the penalty for sin? Who did Jesus die for?
5. What did the just judge say when his beloved mother stood guilty before him as a judge?
6. How is this judge like Jesus?

Phrases to Memorize

1. Jesus Christ is the Son of God and the only one who can save us from going to hell.
2. God is one, but is represented by the Father, the Son, and the Holy Spirit.
3. Jesus, being God, became man and died on the cross in our place.
4. Christ fully paid the penalty for our sins and now we, if we ask God for forgiveness with all our heart, and have faith in Jesus, can be friends of God.
5. God's forgiveness is freely available to all.

Other Bible passages on the theme for reading and memorization

Rom. 5:6-8; Acts. 4:12; Mt. 3:13-17; Eph. 2:8-10; Heb. 9:27; Rom. 5:12; Jn. 3:16; Acts. 3:19.

6

How to Become a Child of God

Memorize

John 1:12 "But to all who believe him and accepted him, he gave the right to become children of God."

God not only wants you to be His friend and receive His love, but he also wants to make you His son or daughter. Can you imagine what a great privilege it will be to be a son or daughter of God?! In this lesson, I will show you how you can become a son or daughter of God. These instructions are in the Bible, and if we follow them, God will do His part. Being a son or daughter of God means that God puts a very great gift in your hands, this gift is eternal life.

❓ Introductory Questions

> 1. Do you know what eternal life is?
> 2. Why is it so important to have eternal life?
> 3. Do you know who is the only one who can give you the gift of eternal life?

Bible Story (Luke 15:11-32)

Yes, you answered correctly. God, through His Son Jesus, is the only one who can give you eternal life. Adam and Eve had eternal life when they were in the Garden of Eden, but after they sinned, their sin separated them from God, and this separation from God means eternal death. Adam and Eve represent humanity, who, using their right to choose, chose to be separated from God. Now, since Jesus paid for everyone's sin on the Cross, remember?, now each one of us can return to God.

A man had two sons. One day, the younger of them said to him, "Father, give me my inheritance." Then the father was sad, but he gave him the money that was due to him from his inheritance. This son went away and foolishly spent all the money, until he no longer had a single cent. So, he went and asked for a job tending pigs, and being hungry, he wanted to eat the food that was given to the pigs. At that moment, this young man began to think: "If I were in my father's house there would be plenty of food, and here I am dying of hunger." Then he also said: "I will go to my father, I will say to him: 'Father, I am sorry for what I did to you, please forgive me. Take me in and make me at least as one of your humble slaves.'" When this young man did this, his father welcomed him with joy and said: "This is my son who was lost and has now been found."

Illustration

Let's talk about the story of George Müller. George's father was a Christian, and he thought that sending George to a Christian school would help him meet God. Instead, George spent his time with his "friends" gambling, cursing and talking about women. The money he received from his father, he spent on his vices and then went to school and pretended to be a poor boy so that he would be allowed to study for free. But one day, a friend of George's invited him to a prayer meeting. George intended to sow doubt in the hearts of those present, but he couldn't do it. He went back again, and then again. This last time, God touched his heart, he fell on his knees and confessed his sins to the Lord, and asked Jesus to come into his heart. George Müller later became a great missionary who was the director of an orphanage that fed thousands of orphaned children. What Jorge Müller did is what you must do to become a child of God.

Questions About the Class

1. Why could Adam and Eve no longer have eternal life?
2. What did the son who left his father do with the money he gave him?
3. What made the son who left his father come back?
4. What did the son say to his father? What was his attitude when he said it? How did his father receive him?
5. Who was George Müller before he became a Christian?
6. What did George Müller do to change his life? What happened to George Müller's life after he asked God for forgiveness for his sins and asked Jesus to come into his heart?

Phrases to Memorize

1. Jesus Christ is the Son of God and the only one who can save us from going to hell.
2. God is one, but is represented by the Father, the Son and the Holy Spirit.
3. Jesus, being God, became man and died on the cross in our place.
4. Christ fully paid the debt of our sins and now we, if we ask God for forgiveness with all our heart, and have faith in Jesus, can be friends of God.
5. God's forgiveness is freely available to all.

Actividad

Ask your teacher to help you become a son/daughter of God. You must pray, and in your prayer be sure to mention these things:

1. Lord, I recognize that I am a sinner, I know that I have done wrong before you, and I repent with all my heart.
2. I want you to forgive me now for all the wrong I have done.
3. Your sacrifice on the cross paid for all my sins and I want your precious blood to cleanse me of all evil.
4. I open my heart to your love so that you, who are love, may enter it and dwell there. Fill my heart with your love, for I believe in you.

5. Make me, Lord, I ask you, a son/daughter of God right now, for I believe in you. Jesus, you are my Savior and Lord.

The proof that Jesus really dwells in your heart will be that you begin to tell everyone that Jesus is your Lord and Savior; that is the confession that He expects from you.

Recommendations for those who have just been born again

1. *Attend your church services as much as you can.* It is very important that you listen to the word of God and have fellowship with other Christians.
2. *Read your Bible.* Find a version of the Bible that you can understand well; ask your parents and the pastor for a Bible they recommend.
3. *Talk about Jesus as much as you can.* Tell your friends and family that Jesus is now in your heart, that you have decided to follow Him and this is the most wonderful thing that has happened in your life!
4. *Remember that God is now your heavenly Father, and it is very important to talk to Him daily,* as much as you can. Talking to Dad is the most beautiful thing in life, and true Christians spend as much time as they can talking to their heavenly Father, and they delight in talking to Him.
5. There will always be someone who makes fun of you, *but don't pay attention to them,* that is normal. Those who make fun of you need Jesus. Pray for them, and tell them about God's love.
6. *Listen to Christian music and sing to the Lord with all your heart.* The Lord loves it when we sing to Him.
7. If you do something that you know you shouldn't do, *ask God for forgiveness immediately* and move on. You should ask God in prayer to help you overcome all evil.
8. *Find a counselor.* The person who is giving you these classes is possibly the best person to help you walk in the Christian life. Tell him or her that you want to learn to serve the Lord Jesus.

Other Bible passages on the theme for reading and memorization

Rom. 10:9; Rev. 3:20; Acts. 16:31; Mk. 16:16; Rom. 14:11; Rom. 15:9; 1 Jn. 1:9.

PART II. DOCTRINE

7

If Jesus Dwells in Your Heart, You Will Speak of Him

Memorize

Luke 12:8 "I tell you, whoever publicly acknowledges me before others, the Son of Man will also acknowledge before the angels of God".

The first thing a baby does when it is born is cry, and when it cries, the doctors say: "It is alive!" This is a kind of "confession" and proof that this baby has been born alive. In the same way, the proof that Christ has really entered your heart is that you will tell everyone what has happened to you. You will confess Christ in front of other children or teenagers: you will be able to tell them that Jesus now lives in your heart! That is the confession that God expects to see in you. If you are afraid to talk about the Lord, and you are not able to talk about Jesus to your friends and family, then it means that you have not yet given your life completely to the Lord Jesus.

❓ Introductory Questions

1. What do you say to people when you talk to them about Jesus?
2. Why do you think that telling everyone that you love Jesus is so important to God?
3. What happened to all the early Christians who confessed that Jesus was their Savior and Lord? Can you imagine? What experiences have you had when you have confessed Jesus in front of your friends and family? Tell us about your experience.

Bible Story (Mark 5:1-20)

One day Jesus and his disciples were sailing on the Sea of Galilee and when they reached the shore, in a region called Gadara, something extraordinary happened. A very strange man came to Jesus. This was a man who was very dirty, without clothes, and his skin was wounded and full of scars. The local people had tried to tie him up, but he was so strong that he could break even chains. He lived in the cemetery and was a terrifying person: he was full of demons. Do you know what that is? Did you know that a person without Christ can be possessed by demons?

Now when Jesus arrived, the man knelt down. Jesus asked the demons what their names were. They said their name was Legion. In Jesus' time, a large group of soldiers (sometimes there were more than 6,000) was called a "legion." In other words, this poor man was possessed by thousands of demons. But Jesus drove them out with one word. Then the man was free and able to think clearly. He put on clothes and wanted to go with Jesus. But Jesus said to him, "Go home to your own people and tell them how great things the Lord has done for you and how he has had mercy on you."

Illustration

Fanny Crosby was a Christian songwriter. She went blind as a baby, but God gave her an extraordinary talent for writing hymns and Christian songs. She loved to talk about Jesus. When someone asked her how she came to write a beautiful song called Rescuing the Perishing, she said that she wrote it after talking to some boys about Jesus Christ. "One of those days," she continued, "I felt the need to say, 'Here's a boy who wants to meet his mother in heaven, but the only way that will be possible is by meeting Jesus.'" When she finished speaking, a young boy approached her and said, "I guess that's what you said; I don't know how you knew, but a few years ago my mother died, and I promised her that I would meet her in heaven. However, my life is far from God, and now I'm sure that I will never be able to keep my promise if I don't get closer to Jesus. Could you help me?" That day, Fanny Crosby helped that boy meet the Lord Jesus. He asked God for forgiveness for his sins and confessed Him as his Savior and Lord. Then the young boy said joyfully: "Now I know that I will meet my mother in heaven, because I have met God."

❓ Questions About the Class

1. What happened when Jesus arrived in the region of Gadara?
2. How do you describe the demon-possessed man? What was he like? What was he like when Jesus found him?
3. How did Jesus cast out the demons in the man?
4. What did Jesus say to the man after he was freed?
5. Who was Fanny Crosby?
6. What did Fanny Crosby love to do?
7. Why did the young boy Fanny spoke to say that he could not meet his mother in heaven?

Phrases to Memorize

1. Jesus is now the most important person in my life and I want everyone to know that.
2. I will tell all my friends how wonderful Jesus is and the peace and joy I now feel knowing that my sins have been forgiven and that I have entry into heaven through the precious blood of Jesus.
3. Testifying about Jesus is a great joy and blessing.
4. Helping others encounter Jesus is the best way to show them love.

Other Bible passages on the theme for reading and memorization

1 Pet. 3:15; Mk. 16:15-16; Col. 4:6; Rom. 1:16; Mt. 5:16; Mt. 28:18-20; Acts. 1:8; Lk. 24:46-49; 2 Cor. 5:18-21; Rom. 10:14; Acts. 22:15; Acts. 4:20; Mt. 5:15; Acts. 10:42.

8

Seeing the Face of Jesus Every Day

Memorize

Psalms 116:2 "Because he has inclined his ear unto me, therefore will I call upon him as long as I live."

When you become a son or daughter of God, you now have a great privilege: prayer. Prayer is talking to God through Jesus. Because you have believed in Jesus Christ and accepted Him as your Savior and Lord, you can now talk to Jesus' Father (who is also now your Heavenly Father), and you can talk to Him with confidence. Every Christian has the privilege (but also the responsibility) to pray every day and constantly. In Matthew 6:9-13 and Luke 11:2-4 Jesus teaches us to pray.

? Introductory Questions

1. What do you think Jesus wants you to pray for?
2. Do you think praying is like talking to your mom or dad? Yes/no, why?
3. Why do you think praying is so important to God?
4. Think about the best Christian you know. Do you think he or she prays a lot? Do you think the more you pray, the better Christian you will be?

Bible Story (Luke 18:1-8)

What characterizes all the greatest Christians in history is that they read their Bibles a lot and prayed to God every day. Many of them spent many hours on their knees praying. God wants us to spend a lot of time before Him praying. Can you imagine if we just needed to say one sentence, and God would answer immediately? So, in order for something to happen, He wants us to insist and talk to Him a lot in private; in this way, He will come, extend His hand of mercy, and help us. Jesus' public prayers were very short, but they were backed up by many hours of secret prayer.

On one occasion, Jesus told the story of a widow who wanted a judge to give her justice, since there was a person who was always doing her wrong. The problem was that this judge was a bad and unjust judge, and every time the widow came, he did not want to help her at all. He preferred to serve the rich and powerful, but this widow (and normally widows in Jesus' time were very poor), he did not want to serve her. However, she continued to come to him and insisted. She was so persistent that this judge, because of how annoying this widow was to him, finally helped her. Jesus said that God is not unjust, but kind and compassionate, then he asked: "And will God not give justice to his chosen ones, who cry out to him day and night? Will he delay in answering them?" God wants us to pray constantly and insist until we receive His answer.

Illustration

Roger Steer wrote the following account in his book *George Müeller: Delight in God*: There was one occasion when George Müller, a man well known for his life of prayer, was sailing to Quebec. As he boarded, Mr. Müller said to the captain, "I need to get to Quebec by Saturday afternoon." The captain, at Müller's words, with a small smile replied, "Excuse me, but that will be impossible. Have you seen the thick fog out there?" "No," George Müller replied, "but my eyes are not on the fog, but on God, who controls everything in the universe. For 57 years I have never broken an engagement, and this will be no exception. Let us pray." So they went down to the chart room, and there, in front of the captain, George Müller knelt down, prayed a simple prayer, stood up, and before the captain could also pray, he said to him: "Since you do not believe, there is no need for you to pray." Then he told the captain to go up and see that the fog was no longer there. The captain went up and sure enough, the fog was gone! That was how Müller kept his promise.

Every time you and I pray, we must have faith; that is the prayer that God will hear.

Questions About the Class

1. What did the widow want from the unjust judge?
2. Why did the widow need to insist? Why do we also need to insist to God?
3. What is the most important ingredient when praying to God?
4. Why did George Müller want to arrive in Quebec on Saturday afternoon? Why did he not want to wait for the fog to clear?
5. What happens when we have the support of a long time of prayer?
6. What happened when George Müller prayed to God?
7. How many years did George Müller have without breaking a commitment? Do you think it is important for a Christian to keep a promise?

Phrases to Memorize

1. I will pray every day of my life without fail. God expects me to speak to Him constantly.
2. Every time I pray, I will pray with faith, because God always keeps His word and keeps it. I must also keep my word.
3. God expects me to insist in my prayer and not be discouraged in continuing to pray.
4. If I manage to have a powerful prayer life, my public prayers will be short and will always move the hand of God.

Other Bible passages on the theme for reading and memorization

1 Jn. 5:14-15; 1 Chr. 16:11; 2 Chr. 6:21, 7:14; Eph. 6:18; Jer. 29:12-13; Job 22:27; Jas. 5:13; Mk. 11:24; Mt. 5:44; Mt. 6:7; Mt. 26:41; Rom. 12:12; Ps. 4:1; Ps. 145:18; Mt. 7:11; Lk. 6:12; Lk. 18:1; Rom. 8:26; Phil. 4:6.

9

Jesus Rose Again on the Third Day

Memorize

Acts 3:14-15 "But you denied the Holy and Righteous One, and asked for a murderer to be granted to you, and you killed the Author of life, whom God raised from the dead. To this we are witnesses."

Christ truly died on the cross and was buried, but God raised Him up on the third day, just as Jesus had said. The resurrection of our Lord Jesus is the greatest miracle ever performed, and it is our greatest victory as well. The apostle Paul said that if Jesus had not been resurrected, our faith would be of no use (1 Cor. 15:14, 17). Likewise, He has promised that one day, when we die, we will also be resurrected to be with Him for eternity.

❓ Introductory Questions

1. What would have happened if Christ had not been resurrected? What do you think? (Read 1 Cor. 15:14, 17 again).
2. Why can you be sure that Jesus really was resurrected?
3. If Christ has been resurrected, it means that He conquered _____. (The answer is in the story).

Bible Story (Matthew 28:1-10; John 20:1-29)

Death is man's number one enemy, and the Bible also calls it the last enemy (1 Cor. 15:26). If Christ had not been resurrected, we would not be able to enter heaven. Why? Because, even though Jesus Christ died for us, God the Father needed to accept that sacrifice, and the resurrection has that meaning. It is as if you have already done a task, but you need to hand it in and have your teacher accept it, otherwise it was useless to have done it, right? So, Jesus' sacrifice had to be accepted. Also, the resurrection means that <u>He conquered death</u>. It also means that we are capable of being united to Christ and that we <u>can be like Him</u>.

Jesus could not be a liar, and He had said that He would rise again. However, after Jesus died, the disciples were very sad, thinking that everything was over. But on Sunday, being the third day since the Lord had died, some women went to the tomb to put perfume on Jesus' body. They were thinking about who would help them move the stone from the tomb, but when they got there, they found that the large stone that was at the mouth of Jesus' tomb had been removed. They thought that someone had stolen Christ's body, but an angel appeared to them and told them that Jesus, who had been crucified, was not there because He had risen from the dead. Then Jesus appeared to them and told them to go tell the apostles. After they went to tell the apostles, Peter and John went to the tomb and found it empty. John went in and found only the linen cloths and the shroud that was on Jesus' head.

Illustration

Buddha was a man who made a religion called Buddhism. This man lived more than two thousand years ago. Many years after Buddha's death, one of his finger bones was sent as a gift to an emperor of China during the Tang Dynasty, but then it was lost and was missing for more than two thousand years. Finally, in 1981, this little bone was found, and this fact made all the Buddhists of the world happy.

We Christians do not look for any bones of our Lord, because they do not exist. He rose from the grave and lives forever and ever.

❓ Questions About the Class

1. Why did Jesus need to be resurrected? (Name three things).
2. Where was Jesus' body placed when He died?
3. What did the women who went to the tomb find?
4. What did the angel say to the women? When Jesus Himself appeared to them, what did He say?
5. What did Peter and John find when they went to the tomb? What did John see when he entered Jesus' empty tomb?
6. How is Christianity different from all other religions?

Phrases to Memorize

1. Jesus needed to be resurrected so that we could enter heaven.
2. Jesus said He would be resurrected, and He kept what He said. So, He will keep all His promises without missing a single one.
3. Just as Jesus conquered death, we are also conquerors over death because one day we will be resurrected as well.
4. Jesus' resurrection caused Jesus to send us the Holy Spirit so that we could live a life close to God, just like Jesus Himself.
5. Jesus' resurrection fulfilled the Old Testament prophecies that say He would be resurrected.

Other Bible passages on the theme for reading and memorization

Rom. 4:25; Acts. 2:24; 1 Cor. 15:55-57; 2 Cor. 4:14; Rom. 6:4, 8; Job 19: 25; Is, 53: 10-12; Rom. 1:4; Acts. 2:33; 1 Pet. 1:3-4; 1 Cor. 15:20-22; Acts. 17:30-31.

10

The Bible is the Truth

Memorize

John 5:39 "You search the Scriptures because you think that in them you have eternal life; and it is they that bear witness about me."

Now you know that God is the Creator, that He wants to be your friend, and that He loves you. You also know that man has sinned and that Jesus Christ is the solution to his great problem; that He died, but He also rose again. Now you have also opened your heart to God's love, you have asked for forgiveness, and you have trusted in Jesus Christ as your only and sufficient Savior and Lord. Now, you have surely noticed that we have been constantly opening the Bible. The Bible is God's revelation to man; it is the Word of God.

❓ Introductory Questions

1. Do you know how many books there are in the Bible? How many books are in the Old Testament and the New Testament?
2. Why is it so important for a Christian to read his/her Bible every day?
3. How can a person understand the Bible?

Bible Story (Acts 8:26-40)

There was in the church of Jerusalem (this church was the first Christian church) a very outstanding disciple (a follower of Jesus) named Philip. This disciple had a very beautiful ministry: the evangelization of the lost. He went to Samaria (a region near Jerusalem), preached Christ and many believed in the Lord and were healed of their diseases.

When Philip was there, the Holy Spirit (remember, He is the third person of the Holy Trinity) led Philip to a place where an African was reading the Bible. This African (from Ethiopia) was a very important person in the government of his country. When Philip saw him, this man was sitting in his chariot reading the Bible, but he could not understand what he was reading. He was reading a passage from Isaiah 53 where it says: "He was led like a sheep to the slaughter, And like a lamb before its shearer, mute, So he did not open his mouth. In his affliction he was not vindicated, But who can declare his generation? For his life has been taken from the earth." Then the Holy Spirit said to Philip, "Go near that chariot." When Philip came near, he asked him, "Do you understand what you are reading?" And the Ethiopian African answered, "How can I, unless someone teaches me?" Then Philip showed him that this passage is talking about Jesus, who died like a lamb. He is the Lamb of God. Reading the Scriptures was very important for this man to get to know Jesus Christ; the same is true for all of us.

Illustration

In 1914, Ernest Shackleton and a team of explorers set out for Antarctica to accomplish a feat never before accomplished: to cross Antarctica from one side to the other via the South Pole. When they reached the Antarctic continent (Antarctica), their ship became trapped in the ice, and they could go no further. They only had one small lifeboat that could fit five people. It was then that they made the decision that five of them would row back in that small boat 1,280 km (800 miles) to Georgia Island, where they could find help, while the rest would stay on Elephant Island. The journey was the most dangerous and challenging one there could be, with treacherous seas and storms with giant waves, and the chances of survival were very small. But they, using only a compass and a sextant (navigational instrument) and rowing for 15 days, were able to reach the island of Georgia and return in a boat to rescue the rest of the team. All were eventually saved. This story teaches us that in the Christian life there will be many storms, but the Bible is the Christian's compass.

Questions About the Class

1. What was the Ethiopian doing when Philip first saw him?
2. Who was the passage the Ethiopian was reading about?
3. What did Philip do to help the Ethiopian?
4. Why is it so important for a Christian to read the Bible every day?
5. What would have happened if those who returned for help in the illustration story had not had a compass?
6. How is the compass in the story similar to the Bible and the Christian?

Phrases to Memorize

1. The main theme of the Bible is the love of God through Jesus Christ.
2. You and I need to read the Bible every day to maintain our fellowship with Jesus.
3. The Bible is God's wisdom and we need His advice to live successful lives and be powerful on earth.
4. To understand the Bible we need the help of the Holy Spirit and other "Philips" (other Christians) to help us.
5. The Bible is the Word of God and is the only means to obtain faith: "So then faith comes by hearing, and hearing by the word of God" (Rom. 10:17).

Other Bible passages on the theme for reading and memorization

2 Ti. 3:16-17; Rom. 10:17; Mt. 24:35; Is. 40:8; Is. 55:11; Jer. 23:29; Dt. 8:3; Mt. 4:4; Jos. 1:8; Ps. 119:105; Ps. 19:7-11; Ps. 119:9; Jn. 17:17.

11
Jesus Continues to Heal the Sick

Memorize

Isaiah 53:5 "But he was wounded for our transgressions, he was bruised for our iniquities: the chastisement of our peace was upon him; and with his stripes we are healed."

Chastisement: severe punishment.

Jesus Christ is the same yesterday, today, and forever. The same Jesus we read about in the Bible is the same today, and He is our healer, not only of the soul but also of the physical body. You see, this verse you have memorized tells us that when Jesus died on the cross, He not only paid for our sins but also for our diseases. It is very important that you believe that Jesus Christ is also the Healer of your physical body.

❓ Introductory Questions

1. Why does Jesus want his children to be healthy?
2. What do you think it means that we were already healed or cured when Jesus died? (quote the opening Bible verse).
3. Do you think Jesus wants to save some people and not others? What is the reason why there are many who are not Christians yet?

Bible Story (Matthew 8:1-3)

Jesus wants His children to be healthy, so He paid the price not only for their sins but also for their illnesses. Jesus always wants to heal everyone, but just as He wants everyone to enter heaven, but not everyone will be able to enter because not everyone believes in Him, the same thing happens with the healing of the body. Jesus expects you and I to believe that He is also our only and sufficient healer; and to believe that His wounds have already made us whole.

God's children are like an army. Imagine what would happen if an army was made up of sick soldiers. Do you think they could win the battles? No! Of course not! There is also a very strong connection between our soul and our physical body. God wants us to be healthy so that we can serve Him with all our strength (read Dt. 6:5; Mk. 12:30).

Every person who came to Jesus for healing was healed by Him; so today, every person who comes to Jesus and believes in Him, Jesus will heal them. We don't know why some people are not healed (even though they say they believe in Jesus for healing), but you and I need to believe what the Bible says and not rely on people's experiences. You see, a man had doubts about whether Jesus wanted to heal him or not. He was a leper. Do you know what a leper is? Leprosy is a skin disease. Well, when he asked Jesus if He wanted to heal him, Jesus answered him vigorously: "I do want to; be clean!" And instantly his leprosy disappeared. Jesus always wants to heal you, but He is waiting for you and me to really believe that He is our Healer and our heavenly Physician.

Illustration

When I was a child (maybe about the same age as you are), my father (who was the pastor of a small church), an evangelist, and I went to pray for an elderly woman. God was using this evangelist mightily to heal the sick, and the elderly woman —who was about 80 years old— had two types of cancer. The doctors had told her that she couldn't possibly live and had sent her home to spend her last days.

The evangelist and we prayed for her on that occasion, and then we went again. What happened next was amazing: she went to church and showed the evidence of the healing she had received from Jesus. Jesus healed her completely! This old woman lived for several more years and was a living testimony of the power of God. Jesus Christ is the same yesterday, today, and forever!

❓ Questions About the Class

1. Jesus paid the price, not only for our sins, but also for our _____.
2. What is needed on our part to receive healing from Jesus?
3. What do we need to base our faith on, the experiences of others or what the Bible says?
4. What did Jesus say to the leper who asked if He wanted to heal him or not?
5. The old woman in the story had two types of cancer. What happened to her?
6. Is the Jesus who walked this earth healing the sick different from the one today? Yes/no, explain.

Phrases to Memorize

1. Jesus Christ died for my sins and also for my illnesses.
2. God's will is always to heal me, but I need to believe that He is my divine Doctor.
3. It is not a sin to go to an earthly doctor, and doctors here do what they can for people to help them; but I have the privilege of having Jesus himself be my Doctor.
4. It is very important to stay healthy, so I must be a good steward of the body that God has given me to take care of.
5. When I read the stories of Jesus' healings, I believe that Jesus is still the same and continues to heal the sick, and will do so until the end of the world.
6. The Bible shows many passages that speak of the healing of the body, and this means that it is very important for God that his children are healthy.

Other Bible passages on the theme for reading and memorization

1 Pet. 2:24; Jas. 5:14-15; Heb. 11:6; 13:8; Ps. 103:1-5; Mt. 8:16-17; Acts. 10:38; Exo. 15:26; Mk. 16:17-18; Acts. 28:8; Rom. 10:17; Mk. 11:24; Lk. 10:9; Jer. 17:14; Exo. 23:25; Acts. 14:8.

12

Jesus baptizes in the Holy Spirit

Memorize

Matthew 3:11 "I baptize you with water for repentance, but he who is coming after me is mightier than I, whose sandals I am not worthy to carry. He will baptize you with the Holy Spirit and fire."

Now Jesus Christ is your Savior and Lord and you have decided to be a Christian. Did you know that Jesus has prepared great gifts for you that He wants to give you? In the previous lesson we saw that He wants you to be healthy and strong physically, but He also wants you to be baptized in the Holy Spirit. The baptism in the Holy Spirit is very important for you to speak the word of God to others with great courage and power; it is also very important for you to serve Christ successfully. In this lesson you will learn what the baptism in the Holy Spirit is.

Introductory Questions

1. Do you know what baptism is?
2. The Holy Spirit is also the Spirit of love. What does God love?
3. Why do you think Jesus wants to baptize you with the Holy Spirit?

Bible Story (Acts 19:1-7)

Baptism means that you are immersed from head to toe in something, such as water. When John the Baptist baptized people, they confessed their sins and gave their hearts to God. But then Jesus came, and John said that He would do something even greater: He would immerse believers in the Holy Spirit. This means that God wants to fill you with His love for the lost and with the power to preach God's Word to them.

The way you can be baptized in the Holy Spirit is simply to ask Jesus with all your heart and to insist and insist until He gives you His great gift. You can also ask another Christian who has already been baptized to pray for you. You will know that He has baptized you because you will begin to speak a new language, which God will give you. When you read the Book of Acts you will realize that this baptism is something that God gives after a person has believed in Jesus. This is what happened to some Christians who were in a city called Ephesus. When the apostle Paul visited them, the first question he asked them was this: "Did you receive the Holy Spirit when you believed in Jesus?" But they did not know that Jesus had this gift for them; but when they found out, Paul prayed for them and they received the baptism in the Holy Spirit and began to speak the new language that God gave them.

Illustration

There was a mighty man of God named Charles Finney. Charles Finney now tells us of his experience of his baptism in the Holy Spirit. He says: "When I closed my office door, I seemed to find myself face to face with the Lord Jesus Christ. I seemed to see Him as I would see another man. He said nothing, but He looked at me in such a way that I fell at His feet. I fell at His feet, and cried aloud like a child, and made confessions as I could in my choked voice. I seemed to have bathed His feet with my tears. I must have been there a good while. I returned to the main office afterward, but when I turned back and was about to sit down, I received the mighty baptism in the Holy Spirit. At that time no one knew about it, but that day the Holy Spirit came upon me in such a way that waves of liquid love seemed to come upon me; it seemed the very breath of God in me. I cried aloud for joy and love."

Questions About the Class

1. What does it mean to be baptized in the Holy Spirit?
2. What happens when you are baptized in the Holy Spirit?
3. What does it take for you to be baptized in the Holy Spirit?
4. What was the first question Paul asked the Christians in Ephesus?
5. What do you remember happening in Charles Finney's experience of being baptized in the Holy Spirit?
6. Charles Finney mentions that he received waves of what?

Phrases to Memorize

1. Jesus Christ wants to baptize me in the Holy Spirit today.
2. To receive the baptism in the Holy Spirit I need to desire it with all my heart and ask the Lord for it insistently.
3. When I receive the baptism in the Holy Spirit, God fills me with His love for the lost and I have power to preach the Word of God to them and serve Jesus more strongly.
4. The sign that I have been baptized in the Holy Spirit will be that I will begin to speak a new language unknown to me, which God will give me.
5. Jesus baptized the disciples with the Holy Spirit and wants to baptize me, because He promised that baptism for all who believe in Him.

Other Bible passages on the theme for reading and memorization

1 Cor. 12:13; Acts. 2:28; Acts. 1:8; Acts. 1:5; Mt. 3:11; Acts. 4:31; Lk. 3:16; Acts. 2:4; Jn. 1:33; Mk. 1:8; Lk. 24:49; Rom. 8:26; Jn. 7:37-39; Acts. 10:34-46. Acts. 10:47.

13

John baptizes Jesus in the Jordan

Memorize

Acts 10:47 "Can any man forbid water, that theses should not be baptized, which have received the Holy Ghost as well as we?"

In addition to the baptism in the Holy Spirit, there is another baptism that those who have believed in Christ receive: water baptism. Water baptism is a commandment of the Lord Jesus Christ that serves as a sign for someone who has decided to follow Him all the days of his/her life. Baptism is a public declaration of your belief in Jesus as your Savior and your commitment to walk alongside Him forever.

❓ Introductory Questions

1. Do you want to follow Jesus by obeying Him every day of your life?
2. Are you willing to even die if necessary for the love of Jesus? When do you think that following Jesus could cost you your life?
3. Do you know that Jesus himself was baptized? Why do you think Jesus Christ himself was baptized?

Bible Story (Matthew 3:13-17)

When you are baptized in water, you are expressing your decision not to offend God in any way. You declare yourself dead to sin. You are willing to obey and love Christ forever. Baptism is like your wedding day with Jesus; it is a very important day in your life. Those who do not wish to publicly testify their love for Jesus with all their heart and their complete belief in Him will not be able to enter heaven. Therefore, water baptism holds significant importance.

Baptism in water is so important that Jesus himself was baptized to set an example for all of us. While John the Baptist was baptizing in the Jordan River, Jesus came to him and asked to be baptized. John did not want to baptize Jesus, since baptism is for those who have repented of their sins and Jesus had no sin; however, Jesus told him that this was necessary. So, John baptized Him. What happened next is that Jesus prayed, and the heavens were opened to Him. The Holy Spirit descended upon Him (that is, He was baptized in the Holy Spirit there), and a voice was heard from heaven (the Father) saying: "This is my beloved Son, in whom I am well pleased."

Illustration

From the time of the apostles and for the next two centuries, water baptism was an open declaration that the believer in Jesus identified himself completely with that despised and hated group of people called Christians. To identify himself as a Christian meant persecution and often even death. It meant being ostracized by your family and rejected by your friends. As long as a person was associating with Christians he was tolerated, but once he was baptized, he was thereby declaring to the whole world, "I belong to that despised group called Christians." Immediately after that happened, that person was persecuted, hated, and mistreated.

Baptism means formally entering the body of Christ (the church is also called *the body of Christ*).

❓ Questions About the Class

1. Why is it necessary to be baptized in water?
2. What does baptism have to do with sin?
3. What can baptism be compared to according to the lesson?
4. Why was Jesus himself baptized?
5. What happened when Jesus was baptized?
6. What happened to the first Christians when they were baptized?

Phrases to Memorize

1. When I am baptized, I am declaring that it is my decision to follow Jesus every day of my life.
2. By being baptized, I totally renounce sin and decide to live only to obey Christ.
3. With baptism, I formally enter the body of Christ, which is the Church.
4. Jesus himself was baptized to leave us an example and received God's praise for it, so I will receive God's praise for that decision.
5. Those who do not want to be baptized (having the opportunity to do so) cannot enter heaven because they do not want to seriously commit themselves to Jesus.
6. With baptism I am also saying that I am willing to die if necessary for the love of Jesus, my Lord and Savior.

Other Bible passages on the theme for reading and memorization

1 Pet. 3:21; Acts. 2:38; Acts. 22:16; Mk. 16:16; Jn. 3:5; Rom. 6:3-4; Mt. 28:18-20; Col 2:12; Rom. 6:3; Acts. 2:41; Acts. 10:47; Acts. 18:8; Eph. 4:5; Acts. 8:38; Mk. 1:4; Tit. 3:5.

14
Christ is Coming Soon

Memorize

Acts 1:11 "'Men of Galilee,', they say, 'why do you stand here looking into the sky? This same Jesus, who has been taken from you into heaven, will come back in the same way you have seen him go into heaven.'"

When Jesus died and rose again, He ascended to His Father and sat at His right hand in heaven. But before He went there, while He was still on earth, He promised to return. Then, at the very moment when Jesus was ascending, a cloud took hold of Him, an angel appeared and said to the disciples those words that you have memorized from Acts 1:11. All Christians believe what Jesus said, and every day we are waiting for Him to return. He promised that He will return without warning us beforehand, therefore, we must always be prepared.

❓ Introductory Questions

1. Why do you think Jesus didn't say the day he would return?
2. What excites you the most when you think that Jesus will return one day? Do you think Jesus will return very soon, for example, that it could be today? Yes/no, why?
3. Imagine what will happen in the world when Jesus returns for us. How do you imagine it will be?

Bible Story (Matthew 25:1-13)

On several occasions Jesus said that after He left, He would return for His disciples; for this reason, Jesus' disciples preached that Jesus was going to return, because He promised it. But Jesus always, when He spoke about this, also warned: "You have to be prepared, because I will not tell you when I am coming!"

To illustrate this, Jesus told the story of ten virgins who were waiting for the bridegroom, who would come at any moment and open the door for them to enjoy the wedding. They wanted to go into the wedding and were waiting outside until the bridegroom came and opened the door for them. But it was nighttime and very dark, and the bridegroom had given them strict orders not to let their lamps go out. Of these ten virgins, five were very diligent and had brought with them enough oil for the whole night; but the other five thought it was not necessary to bring so much. Then the bridegroom took longer than they thought, and they ran out of oil. They wanted to borrow some from the other five, but they needed their own oil; so, they went to buy more. But as they went, the bridegroom arrived and only the five who were ready went into the wedding. Then Jesus finished the story by telling his disciples that they needed to be prepared. All Christians need to always live close to Jesus and without sin: this is what it means to be "ready." Oil is a symbol of the Holy Spirit, who helps us to live without sin.

Illustration

A school principal visited one of the classrooms whose students were the messiest in the school. He talked to the students and made a promise: "I'm going to leave, but I'll be back, and the child I find sitting neatly with his desk clean and tidy, I'll give him a prize." Then one of the children asked, "But when will you be back?" "Oh, I can't tell you that," the principal replied. Then he left.

After he left, a girl said in front of everyone: "I am going to win the prize." "You?" her classmates mocked her. "But you are the messiest in the group." "Yes, but I will have everything in order in the morning," she said. "What if the principal comes at noon?" they asked. "Then I will keep everything clean and in order until noon." "But what if he comes at the end of the day, when we are already going home?" another asked. "Mmm," the girl thought for a moment. "I know!" she finally answered. "I will keep everything clean and in order all day, and then I will win the prize."

Questions About the Class

1. What did the girls in the Bible Story want?
2. What was the difference between them?
3. What does it mean to "be prepared"?
4. What does the oil in the Bible Story symbolize?
5. What did the girl in the illustration have to do to win the prize?
6. What did the girl decide to do in the end? How is the story in the illustration similar to the Christian life?

Phrases to Memorize

1. It is wonderful to think that Jesus will one day return for me.
2. Jesus promised to return and He will keep His promise.
3. No one knows when Jesus will return, because He said it would be a surprise.
4. It is very important that I be prepared for Jesus' coming, because I do not want to be left behind when He returns.
5. "Being prepared" means living life close to Jesus, not doing anything that offends Him, and doing what He wants.
6. Every day I will ask the Holy Spirit for help to keep me from offending Jesus, and to stay close to Him, doing what God wants.

Other Bible passages on the theme for reading and memorization

Mt. 24:36; 1 Ts. 4:16-17; Rev. 22:12-13; Jn. 14:3; Mt. 24:31-33; 1 Cor. 14:52; Acts. 1:11; Rev. 3:11; Rev. 22:7; Jas. 5:9; Rom. 13:11; 1 Cor. 16:22; Tit. 2:13.

15

Dinning with Jesus

Memorize

1 Corinthians 11:24 "This is my body, which is for you; do this in remembrance of me."

It was very important for Jesus to shed His blood, because His precious blood cleanses our hearts from all sins (yours and those of everyone else). Furthermore, His body, when He died on the cross, was very mistreated: they whipped Him, put a crown of thorns on His forehead, nailed His hands and feet to the wood of the cross with thick steel nails. And finally, they pierced His body near the ribs with a lance (in the side). Christ wanted us Christians to constantly remember how important His death was.

❓ Introductory Questions

1. Why do you think it is so important to remember the death of the Lord Jesus as much as possible?
2. Do you think this is a command from Jesus or just something optional?
3. Only those who have been baptized can take the Holy Supper, do you know why?

Bible Story (Matthew 25:1-13)

The Holy Supper is an act to remember and meditate on the death of Jesus, and this brings much good for each one, because the death of Jesus unites us with God and keeps us united to the church (the other Christians). The death of Jesus made sin be erased from our hearts and thus, by being clean before God, we can have communion with Him. Remember that God detests sin and only if we are clean from it, can we be close to Him. He will dine with us if we remain holy. The Holy Supper has two main requirements: the first is to be baptized, because that means that you have publicly confessed to being a follower of Jesus; and the second is to ask for forgiveness and forgive all those whom you have offended or who have offended you. God wants you to forgive with all your heart those who have offended you, because if you do not, He will not forgive you either; and also, that you ask for forgiveness from those whom you have offended.

Jesus told his disciples to prepare a place to dine together. When they were there, He broke the bread, gave it to them, and told them that it symbolized his body, which would suffer greatly. Then he told them to also drink the drink made from grapes, which symbolizes His precious blood, shed for us. Dining together brings unity, because in Jesus we are all brothers. God wants us to have love and be at peace with everyone at all times. Judas was there, and he dined too, but then he ended up very badly; likewise, those who take the Holy Supper without fulfilling God's requirements can also end up very badly.

Illustration

An old tradition of Jews living in other countries is that after eating at their traditional Passover feast, they raise a glass of grape juice and everyone says, "Next time in Jerusalem." They say this because they look forward to one day returning to their homeland and celebrating this traditional feast in their own country.

The celebration of the Lord's Supper is intended to remember Jesus' death until He comes, that is, until His return. And we, when we celebrate the Holy Supper, have the hope of one day celebrating it together in our homeland: in heaven.

❓ Questions About the Class

1. Why does taking the Holy Supper bring us much good? (as seen in this lesson)
2. Can we dine with Jesus if we practice sin? Yes/no, why?
3. What are the two requirements to celebrate the Holy Supper according to the lesson?
4. Why is forgiving others so important to God?
5. What does the bread and the drink made of grapes symbolize in the Holy Supper?
6. What can happen if someone takes the Holy Supper without fulfilling God's requirements?
7. What is the hope we have in taking the Holy Supper?

Phrases to Memorize

1. I must be very respectful when I take the Holy Communion, because the bread symbolizes the body of Christ, and the drink made from grapes symbolizes the precious blood of Jesus.
2. I must take the Holy Communion as often as possible, because it brings me blessing.
3. The main purpose of the Holy Communion is to have peace with my brothers and to love them with all my heart, remembering that the death of Jesus brought me peace with God.
4. Taking the Holy Communion is not something optional but something obligatory for all Christians.
5. God wants to bless my soul and my body, and when I take the Holy Communion, I remember that the death of Jesus has brought me blessing for my soul and for my body.

Other Bible passages on the theme for reading and memorization

1 Jn. 1:7; Heb. 10:25; 1 Cor. 11:23-27; Mt. 26:26-28; Jn. 6:53-58; Mk. 14:22-25; Gn. 14:18; Lk. 24:13-32; Acts. 2:42; Is. 53:5.

Part III. The Moral Law of God

16

Worship God alone

Memorize

John 4:24 "For God is Spirit, so those who worship him must worship in spirit and in truth."

God commands that you worship only Him and does not allow you to worship anyone or anything else. He is jealous and very strict in this. If you or I worship something other than Him, this is called idolatry, and worshiping an idol means putting something or someone as more important than God. Something that takes over your thoughts and from which you expect to receive what only God can give (peace, security, love, joy, etc.). Also, an idol is something (or someone) you give what only God must receive (the first and best of our time, money, and strength).

❓ Introductory Questions

1. The people of Israel had a lot of problems with idolatry, can you tell us a little about that?
2. What are some things that can be an idol in your life?
3. Do you think that a sport can be an idol? Can school be an idol? A video game?

Bible Story (Luke 12:15-21)

An idol is anything you find purpose and direction in, outside of God. It is what you go to for happiness; it is what causes you to sin; it is what keeps you away from the Bible; it is what keeps you away from prayer; it is what keeps you away from going to God's house; it is what keeps you away from obeying your parents and God. It can also be someone you greatly admire. But the most common example today is the god of money. If you do things only to get money, then it is very possible that this is your god and not the God of the Bible.

Jesus said that this god is called greed (the love of money), and He told the story of a rich man. This rich man had made a great profit in one year, and he didn't know what to do with all that he had. Since he was a farmer and had harvested a lot and had no room for all that he had harvested, he said to himself, "Oh, I know what I will do: I will tear down my barns and make them larger; and then I will say to myself, 'Oh, be merry, eat and drink, you have plenty of money laid up for many years...'" But then God said to him, "You fool! This night you will die, and the things you have laid up, whose will they be?" And then Jesus said, "So it is with the one who lays up treasure for himself and is not rich toward God."

Illustration

An Indian tale tells of four children who each had a dream to fulfill in life. They promised each other to go around the land and fulfill their dream, and then meet again when they grew up. Time passed, and they met to talk about what they could do now.

One said, "If I can find a bone, I can put flesh on it." The second said, "If a bone has flesh, I can put sinews and skin on it." The third said, "If you can show me a bone with flesh, sinews and skin on it, I can make all the parts of the body." And the last said, "I can give it life." "Let us go and find the bone and show what each of us can do." So they went into the forest and found the bone of a lion; and each of them did what he knew how to do. But when the lion came to life, he rushed at them, tore them to pieces and ate them.

This story illustrates that a dream we have can become our idol, and that idol will end up destroying our life, because God does not tolerate us having any God outside of Him.

Questions About the Class

1. Mention at least three things that define what an idol is?
2. What is the most common god in the world today?
3. How can you know that your god is money?
4. What did the rich man who had made a lot of money in one year say?
5. What did God say to the rich man after what he had said?
6. What does the Indian story that serves as the illustration teach us?
7. Are you willing to follow God's purpose for your life and not what the people of the world say?

Phrases to Memorize

1. An idol is anything that occupies my thoughts, separates me from prayer, from the Bible, and from obedience to God and my parents.
2. All the money I earn belongs to the Lord and is only a means to do His will.
3. I will be what God wants me to be and not what society or people, or myself want.
4. I can enjoy and be happy with the things that God gives me, but I put my love only in the One who has given me those things: God.
5. I ask the Lord for forgiveness for any idol in my life, and I cast it out of me in the name of Jesus. Because only the worshipers of the true God can enter heaven.
6. God does not tolerate idolatry and I ask the Holy Spirit for help to protect me from it, and I pray in the name of Jesus.

Other Bible passages on the theme for reading and memorization

Exo. 20:3-6; Jon. 2:8; Col. 3:5; 1 Jn. 5:21; Is. 44:9-20; Gal. 5:19-21; 1 Cor. 10:14; Sal. 16:4; Jer. 11:12; Gal. 4:8; Rev. 9:20; 1 Cor. 10:7; 1 S 15:23; Jer. 7:18; Rom. 1:23; 1 Cor. 6:9; Rev. 21:8; Eph. 5:5.

17 Religious Images

Memorize

Exodus 20:4 "You shall not make unto you any graven image, or any likeness of any thing that is in heaven above, or that is in the earth beneath, or that is in the water under the earth."

In ancient times, when the Old Testament was written many years ago, the people of Israel were surrounded by nations that worshiped idols. These idols were images made of stone, wood, metal, and other materials. They believed that these gods that they had made themselves had power. The Israelites were tempted by these idols, and most of the time they worshiped them instead of God (the true God is invisible). Today there are still many in the world who worship these images; so, humans have this weakness, and God forbids us to use any representation of God (image) to "help" us worship God.

❓ Introductory Questions

1. What kind of images do you know? Where have you seen them?
2. Do you think that these images deserve some kind of respect?
3. Some people simply call religious images "art," but God forbade the creation of such images. Do you know anyone who says that images of saints, Mary, or Jesus are just "art"? What do they say? Why do they say that they are not bad?

Bible Story (Exodus 32:1-10)

God forbids us to make or bow down to any figure that represents God or Jesus (who is God). Likewise, the image of any other person or animal or angel that represents a divine or sacred being (which must be treated with respect).

In the Bible, we have the story of when God gave the Ten Commandments to Moses on Mount Sinai. It turned out that when Moses was on top of the mountain and spent 40 days there talking to God, the people thought that Moses would not return and asked his brother (Aaron) to make them an image to worship. Then Aaron asked them to give him the gold that they had, and he made them a calf with that gold. When the golden calf was raised up, the people said: "Israel, these are your gods, who brought you up from the land of Egypt," so they bowed down to it and worshiped it. When that happened, God, who knows everything, told Moses what was happening, and he came down and severely punished the Israelites for having done something so displeasing in the eyes of God.

Illustration

Hideyoshi was a 16th century Japanese ruler who built a large statue of Buddha inside a temple in the city of Kyoto. It took 50,000 men and five years of work to build it; however, in 1596, immediately after the huge statue was finished, an earthquake occurred, collapsing the roof of the temple and smashing the statue to pieces. Furious, Hideyoshi shot an arrow into the ruins and said, "You cost me so much money, and you can't even take care of your own temple?"

The Word of God says: "Their idols are merely things of silver and gold, shaped by human hands. They have mouths but cannot speak, and eyes but cannot see. They have ears but cannot hear, and noses but cannot smell. They have hands but cannot feel, and feet but cannot walk, and throats but cannot make a sound" (Ps. 115:4-7).

Questions About the Class

1. Why does God forbid us to make images? Is it permitted by God to represent the Father, Jesus, or the Holy Spirit with objects (statues, icons, sculptures, etc.)?
2. What happened to the people of God when Moses spent 40 days on Mount Sinai talking to God?
3. What did the people of Israel say when the golden calf that Aaron had made was set up?
4. What did Moses do when he learned what the people had done?
5. What did the Japanese ruler in the illustration say?
6. Mention at least three things that idols (images) cannot do?

Phrases to Memorize

1. God forbids us to represent Him with any visible image, because He is invisible.
2. Jesus is the only image of God, but no one knows what He was like when He was on earth or what He is like now.
3. Images have no power. and we should not treat them with respect, because they are nothing more than objects made of wood, paper, metal, etc.
4. Bowing down to an image is a grave sin before God.
5. We should avoid those images that the world calls "art."
6. We do not need any representation of God or Jesus to "help" us worship the one true God.

Other Bible passages on the theme for reading and memorization

Exo. 20:4; Col. 1.15; Dt. 4:23-24; Exo. 34:14; Dt. 4:16-18; Lev. 26:1; Ps. 97:7; Is. 44:14-16; Is. 42:8; Rev. 19:19; Is. 44:8-11; Hab. 2:18; Jer. 10:14-15; 1 Cor. 8:4; Acts. 14:10-15.

18
The Name of God is Sacred

Memorize

Deuteronomy 5:11 "You shall not misuse the name of the LORD your God, for the LORD will not hold anyone guiltless who misuses his name".

God commands everyone to have great respect and love for His name. Using God's name for purposes that do not honor Him is a sin before Him. For example, saying that God likes to do things that humans do, trying to compare Him to us (for example, saying that God likes a certain football team); or making jokes or pranks using God's name, or making promises (which we do not intend to keep) or swearing (Christians are forbidden to swear). Even if you say "God bless you" but you do not mean it with all your heart (e.g., just to do business), it is all part of taking God's name in vain.

❓ Introductory Questions

1. Have you heard other children use God's name in some expressions?
2. If God is your friend, can you speak to him exactly as you speak to your friends (for example, if you use a nickname to speak to your friend)? Yes/no, why?
3. What does it mean to you to mention God's name with respect and reverence?

Bible Story (Deuteronomy 1:20-27)

When the Israelites left Egypt, they wandered in the wilderness for only two years and God then gave them the opportunity to enter the promised land. When they were at the border of the land, God told them to go in and take it for themselves; but the Israelites, instead of simply obeying God and taking the land, asked Moses to send spies into the land first.

Moses sent 12 spies to scout the Promised Land, and the spies returned. When they returned, ten of them had a bad report and only two (Joshua and Caleb) spoke well of the land and put their faith completely in God to take it. They were excited thinking that God was very generous and good at giving them such a rich and fertile land. But the other ten (and then all the people) spoke badly, not only of the land (which was a land of giants), but of God himself, and said: "God hates us, that's why He brought us out of Egypt, to kill us at the hands of our enemies." What they said was such a serious sin in the eyes of God, that He made them walk around the desert for 40 years until they all died.

Illustration

Did you know that throughout human history, up until about 1100 AD, all people had only one name (not a surname)? And in biblical times, names always had a meaning. God gives a lot of importance to names, because names are related to each person, to their character. For example, the name Barnabas means *son of consolation*.

Also, it was always said of a person, the son of...; for example, in the Bible, it says: "David son of Jesse; Isaac son of Abraham; Jacob son of Zebedee; Simon son of Jonah, etc." The name of someone was related to his father. The son and the daughter reflected their identity with that of their father. Thus, Jesus is called Son of God. This means that his person is identical to his Father. We are children of God because of Jesus; but Jesus is the only begotten Son of God. Therefore, we reflect the identity of Jesus.

Throughout the Bible we can see that the name of God is something very important. The name of God is holy and sacred. So is the name of Jesus and the Holy Spirit. In the name of Jesus demons and diseases flee.

Questions About the Class

1. What are some examples of what it means to take God's name in vain?
2. How did Joshua and Caleb use God's name?
3. How did the other ten spies and all the people use God's name?
4. What was the result of what the ten spies and all the people said?
5. Why is someone's name so important in the Bible?
6. What is the correct way to use God's name?
7. What happens when we use Jesus' name against sickness and demons?

Phrases to Memorize

1. What we say is very important to God, and we must be very careful when we mention His name.
2. The name of God, Jesus, and the Holy Spirit must always be said with respect and reverence.
3. I must also do everything in my power to ensure that others do not mention God's name in vain.
4. God is pleased when we mention His name to worship Him and to have faith in Him (as was the case with Joshua and Caleb).
5. The name of Jesus of Nazareth is Almighty, and God has told us to use it against demons and sickness.
6. Jesus' most important name is Son of God, and this means that He is equal to God the Father.

Other Bible passages on the theme for reading and memorization

Exo. 20:7; Lev. 24:10-23; Ps. 29:2; Lev. 18:21; Jn. 17:6; Mt. 12.37; Prov. 18:21; Rom. 2.24; 1 Tim 6:1; 2 Pet. 2:2; Mt. 12:36-37; Dt. 5:11; Ps. 139:20; Ez. 39:7; Is. 48:1-2.

19

The Day of Rest

Memorize

Ezekiel 20:12 "Also I gave them my Sabbaths as a sign between us, so they would know that I the LORD made them holy."

When God made the world, the Bible says that He rested from His work. Not because God was tired, but to give us an example. He wanted humans to work six days and rest one day, the seventh day. Not necessarily the Saturday that is on our calendar, but the seventh day from the first day of work, which for us is Sunday. God wants us to dedicate that day exclusively to Him. Every day we worship and honor God, but the seventh day is special: a day that we spend completely occupied with the things of God.

❓ Introductory Questions

1. Do you think that Christian children can or should play on Sunday?
2. What do you think should be done on Sunday if that day is dedicated to the Lord?
3. Why do you think God wanted it to be done this way?

Bible Story (Deuteronomy 1:20-27)

Nehemiah was a great man of God. In his book, each of us can learn many things. One of those things that we can learn from the Book of Nehemiah is to obey God and rest on the seventh day. There it says that he observed how the Israelites made grape juice on that day, and loaded their donkeys with grapes, figs, and other loads. He also observed that there were foreigners who came to sell their goods on that day, and the Israelites went to buy them.

Then Nehemiah ordered the gates of the city to be closed on the seventh day, and after working for six days, he ordered that no one was to work. The merchants came to sell as usual and found the gates closed. Then the next week they came again, and again the gates were closed. Until they realized that they should not come that day, because they would not find customers for their goods.

In Jesus' time, the Pharisees turned this blessing from God into a burden, but the Lord Jesus reminded them that it was not a burden but something created for the benefit of human beings. Jesus also said that on that day we should do good to others (Mt. 12:12).

Illustration

The Israelites were slaves and worked every day. Their work was very hard and difficult, for they had to make bricks and then carry them. Without a day of rest, they lived in suffering. However, God gave them a day to rest. The Sabbath is not a burden to us, but a delight. When we rest from ordinary days of work or school, go to worship God at church, and dedicate the whole day to the Lord, God blesses our body; our mind is fresher, and the rest of the week we have greater strength to study and work.

I remember that ever since I was a child, I never did anything related to school on Sunday. But one day when I was in college, I hadn't studied for an exam scheduled for Monday, so I decided to study on Sunday. That Sunday I spent the whole day studying and I studied very hard. It was a math exam. On Monday I took the exam and a few days later I got the results. I was very surprised: I had gotten the lowest grade on that exam in my entire life as a student. Then I cried out to God and asked for forgiveness for not keeping His day and keeping it holy. God had mercy on me and the professor canceled that exam; then, when we retook it, I got an excellent grade. With this experience, I understood that God wants us to rest on the seventh day and if we do, He will help us on the other six days. The Israelites were very blessed to have a day of rest and so are we.

❓ Questions About the Class

1. What did Nehemiah observe the Israelites doing on the seventh day?
2. What did Nehemiah command to be done?
3. What benefit did the Israelites gain when God commanded them to rest on the seventh day?
4. What should be done on that day that is consecrated to God?
5. What will happen on the days we work if we obey God and honor Him on the seventh day?
6. What happened to me when I decided to study the seventh day instead of worshiping God?
7. What did Jesus say to the Pharisees, who had made the seventh day a burden? (Mention things that Jesus said on that subject).

Phrases to Memorize

1. God gave us the command to rest on the seventh day (after six days of work) so that we could have a better life.
2. God wants us to spend that day doing things that honor Him and to worship Him all day.
3. We worship God every day, but the seventh day is special to Him.
4. If we obey God by resting on the seventh day, He will bless the other six days that we study or work on. Jesus also said that the Sabbath is for doing good (healing the sick, preaching the word of God, or serving the community, for example).
5. **Other Bible passages on the theme for reading and memorization**

Exo. 20:8-11; Mk. 2.27; Lev. 23:3; Gn. 2:3; Is. 58:13; Exo. 20:8; Mt. 5:17-19; Lk. 4:16; Dt. 5:12-15; Lk. 23:56.

20

Honor Thy Father and Thy Mother

Memorize

Ephesians 6:2 "'Honor your father and mother' —which is the first commandment with a promise—."

This means several things: First, it means that we should esteem our parents and express that esteem. Second, we should show reverence to them (the opposite would be to despise and mock them). Third, this commandment means to obey them: to do what they command us and not to do what they forbid us to do (and this obedience should be with joy). Fourth, we should submit to their discipline, listen to and follow their instructions (and do this with gentleness). Fifth, we should be willing to follow their advice (this is especially true in the case of Christian parents). Sixth, when they are older, don't take advantage of what belongs to them, but do everything possible to make their old age comfortable and happy.

❓ Introductory Questions

1. What is the best thing you can say about your father and mother?
2. How do your parents show that they love you? What have you seen in them?
3. What does God promise for all those who honor their parents?

Bible Story (Judges 14:1-20)

Samson is one of the most well-known names in the Bible. You probably know him. Yes, you guessed it! He's that man with big muscles! You see, this man received the great blessing of being a servant of God and bringing freedom to Israel. God also gave him great physical strength, which he was to use to free Israel from its enemies.

However, Samson had one major flaw: he did not follow his parents' advice. He wanted to get married, and like him, one day you will want to get married too, right? Or don't you want to get married one day? Now you may say no, but later you will say yes. But you must marry the right person, and it is better to follow your parents' advice so that you make a very good decision. Samson's parents told him to set his sights on a girl from his own town, Israel, where there were good girls who feared God. However, Samson did not want to obey his parents or follow their advice, and because of this, he had to suffer a lot. The story of Samson is a story of suffering and premature death, that is, before his time. He died very young and had little fruit for God.

Illustration

A trucking company wanted to hire a driver to drive a trailer through a mountainous area. The project manager put out an advertisement and began interviewing candidates. When the first candidate came, he asked him: "If you were the driver we hired, how far would you drive from the edge of the cliff?" "I think a couple of meters from the edge," said the candidate. This meant that he was a very capable person for the job. But the interviewer thanked him and did not hire him. Then another came and asked him the same question. The other replied: "I would drive a meter from the edge" (showing off his skill). Finally, one came along and replied: "I would try to drive as far from the edge as possible." Then the manager told the last one: "The job is yours." Our parents always try to keep us away from danger. They have more experience than we do and we should always follow their advice.

❓ Questions About the Class

1. What blessings did Samson receive? What blessings did Samson receive that you have also received?
2. What was Samson's greatest flaw?
3. Who did Samson want to marry? Why did his parents disagree?
4. What kind of girl did Samson's parents want for him?
5. What happened to Samson for not following his parents' advice?
6. What was the question that the boss who was hiring the driver (the one from illustration) asked the candidates?
7. Who did he finally hire? Why did he hire that last one? What does this story teach us?

Phrases to Memorize

1. God commands us to show appreciation, esteem, and love to our parents.
2. God commands us to show reverence and respect for our parents (it is very wrong to make fun of them or despise them).
3. God commands us to obey what our parents command us to do and to avoid doing what they forbid us to do.
4. God commands us to submit to their rebukes and punishments, and to follow their instructions and advice.
5. God commands us to take care of our parents when they are old and to give them the most comfortable life we can.

Other Bible passages on the theme for reading and memorization

Dt. 5:16; Exo. 20:12; Eph. 6:1-3; Prov. 29:15; Mk. 7:10; Exo. 21:17; Lev. 19:3; Prov. 19:18; Ruth 1:16-17; Col. 3:20; Prov. 20:20; Prov. 30:17; Dt. 21:18-21; Prov. 1:8-9; Mal. 1:6; Rom. 8:15; Mt. 15:4; Mt. 19:19.

21

Thou Shalt Not Kill

Memorize

Matthew 5:22 "But I say to you that everyone who is angry with his brother will be liable to judgment; whoever insults his brother will be liable to the council; and whoever says, 'You fool!' will be liable to the hell of fire."

It is very important to God that we love one another. So important is this to God that He will deny entry to heaven to anyone who does not forgive his brother (sister) any offense. Jesus said that the explanation of God's commandment not to kill is not limited to taking the lives of other human beings, but even to getting angry with someone or calling them a *fool* (ignorant, who knows nothing) and a *fatuous* (dumb). Killing a person is not only taking a knife and killing them at once, but also includes damaging their health. God's prohibition of Thou shalt not kill includes not killing yourself (neither at once, nor slowly).

❓ Introductory Questions

1. How often do you get angry at your little brother or sister or your friend?
2. Have you ever been angry at someone for more than a day? How does that make you feel?
3. What could be examples of slowly killing someone?

Bible Story (2 Samuel 13:1-29)

King David had several sons and daughters. One of those sons was named Amnon, and one of David's daughters was named Tamar (who was the daughter of another woman, not Amnon's own mother). The Bible tells the tragic story of Amnon, who wanted to do something wrong with his little sister; and he was very mean to her, because he wanted to see her without clothes (and this is a very bad thing). When he did this very bad thing, Tamar went screaming into the street, because she had been seriously offended by her half-brother. But she had another brother named Absalom, who was the son of the same mother as her (while Amnon was not).

When Absalom heard that his sister had been wronged, he planned to take revenge and kill his half-brother, Amnon. So, he organized a party to which he invited all the king's sons (including Amnon), and he gave the order to his servants to kill his half-brother Amnon when he was very happy at the party, and they did so.

Illustration

Absalom killed his own brother out of revenge. Many murders that have taken place in the land have been the result of revenge. If you are offended by someone, and you do not forgive immediately, that offense grows in your heart until it may reach the point where you wish that person dead (and this is murder in your heart).

Before Abraham Lincoln became President of the United States, he worked as a lawyer. One day, a man came to him because he wanted to sue his neighbor. This man, who was very upset with his neighbor, saw an opportunity to get back at him because his neighbor owed him $2.50. Since his neighbor was so poor that he didn't have that money, he wanted to put him in jail.

Abraham Lincoln tried to convince the man not to sue his neighbor for such a small amount, but he plaintiff refused. So Lincoln took the case and told him he would charge him $10.00. The vengeful man agreed and paid him on the spot. So Lincoln took the money, gave half of it to the poor neighbor (the defendant) and he paid what he owed. The amazing thing was that the plaintiff man, seeing Abraham Lincoln's action, understood the seriousness of his folly. When a person is angry with his brother, Jesus said, he is guilty of murder (because in his heart, if he had the chance, and there were no consequences for it, he would take him off this earth).

Questions About the Class

1. Why was what Amnon did to her little sister so bad?
2. Why did Absalom want to kill his brother?
3. What should you do immediately when someone offends you?
4. Why does Jesus say that you should not get angry or call another person a fool?
5. Is killing a person just taking their life at once? Does it also include harming their health?
6. Why did the man in the illustration want to put his neighbor in jail?
7. What did Abraham Lincoln do?

Phrases to Memorize

1. God commands us to always be at peace with others. Being angry with your brother is as much for God as taking his life.
2. When someone offends you, you must forgive him immediately, just as God forgives you immediately, and as you would wish someone to forgive you.
3. We must do everything in our power to make a person healthy and strong, this is a demonstration of God's love in us.
4. I must also take care of my own health, because the commandment not to kill includes my own life.

Other Bible passages on the theme for reading and memorization

Exo. 20:13; Dt. 5:17; Mt. 5:21; Rom. 13:9; Jas. 2:11; Mk. 10:19; Lk. 18:20; Gn. 9:6; 1 Jn. 3:15; Gn. 9:5-6; Gn. 6:11, 13.

22
Abortion

Memorize

Exodus 23:7 "Have nothing to do with a false charge and do not put an innocent or honest person to death, for I will not acquit the guilty."

The life of a human being is very important to God. Jesus said that the life of a single human being is worth more than the lives of many animals (e.g. Mt. 10:29-31). So valuable is the life of a human being that God the Father sent his Son Jesus to save it. When does human life begin? The life of a human being begins in the mother's womb, and it is there so tiny that no one can see it; it is so tiny that it can only be seen with the help of a microscope.

God protects human life and forbids its destruction. If someone destroys human life in a mother's womb, the Bible calls that murder. Abortion is very bad before God, because it is killing a human being.

Introductory Questions

1. What do you think happened to you when you were in your mother's womb?
2. Do you think it is good or fair to take the life of someone who is innocent? Yes/no, why?
3. What do you think the word *abortion* means?

Bible Story (Jeremiah 1:4-10)

There was a prophet in the Bible named Jeremiah. He was a great prophet of God whom God used to bring His blessed Word to His people. The prophecies of the prophet Jeremiah are written in the book that bears his name and are words of God of great blessing to all of us.

The Bible says that the prophet Jeremiah was called by God when he was in his mother's womb, when he was being formed there. God saw him, and even though Jeremiah could not yet understand God's voice, the Lord said that he would be His prophet, and that he would take His Word to many people. Later, the prophet Jeremiah was born, and while he was still a boy, God spoke to him again and told him what God had told him when he was in his mother's womb. When God told him what He wanted of him, Jeremiah replied, "Ah! Ah, Lord! Behold, I cannot speak, for I am a child." But God told him that even though he was a child, he would be His prophet. God called Jeremiah when he was in his mother's womb.

Illustration

A professor at a famous medical school had a very interesting question for his students. "We have the following case," he said, "a couple of parents are sick, both with diseases that are transmitted from parents to children and are incurable diseases. They had already had four children. The first was born blind; the second had died at birth; the third was born deaf; and the fourth has tuberculosis. Now the mother is pregnant again. What would you recommend?"

The students gathered in groups to discuss the matter, and after several minutes of discussion, they brought their answer to the professor: "Professor, we have been discussing the matter, and most of us, given the circumstances, would advise the parents to abort the baby."

"Well," said the professor with a certain tone of disgust, "you guys have just killed Beethoven."

IDEA: It would be good to present an audio or video with Beethoven's Symphony 5].

Questions About the Class

1. When was the first time God spoke to and called Jeremiah?
2. What did God say to Jeremiah when he was a boy?
3. What did Jeremiah answer God?
4. When does a person's life begin?
5. What is more important, the life of a human being or an animal? Why?
6. Why would medical students at that famous school recommend that the mother mentioned in the illustration have an abortion?
7. Who was Beethoven?

Phrases to Memorize

1. For God the life of every human being is extremely valuable and so it should be for all of us.
2. Abortion is murder in the eyes of God, and He forbids it: You shall not kill, He has said.
3. Human life begins when the baby is so small that it cannot be seen except with the help of a microscope.
4. In some cases, the person guilty of a serious crime or crimes is sentenced to the death penalty.
5. But it will never be fair to take the life of an innocent being (the one who has not yet been born). This is killing the most innocent being that exists.

Other Bible passages on the theme for reading and memorization

Exo. 23:7; Exo. 20:13; Ps. 139.13-16; Jer. 1:5; Ps. 127:3-5; Prov. 6:16-19; Rom. 1:28-32; Prov. 24:11-12; Mt. 18:14; Is. 5:20; Ecc. 11:5; Ps. 127:3-5; Jas. 5:6.

23

Do not Harm your Body

Memorize

1 Corinthians 6:19 "Don't you realize that your body is the temple of the Holy Spirit, who lives in you and was given to you by God? You do not belong to yourself."

Did you know that someone can kill themselves little by little, and this is also very displeasing in the eyes of God? When the Lord saved you, and you were born again in Jesus, your body is God's property and the temple of the Holy Spirit. Therefore, God wants your body to be holy, that is, to be clean of all disease and to be in good health, therefore, God commands us to take care of our body. Also, a person can be deceived by Satan and think about taking his own life, God forbids this, and a person who does so will go to hell, because he is disobeying God's commandment not to kill human life.

❓ Introductory Questions

1. Do you know anyone who smokes, uses drugs, or eats too much?
2. A lie that satan always tells is this: "Nothing will happen to you." What would you say to him if he told you this when offering you some drugs or a cigarette?
3. Did you know that eating too much every day is another way of killing yourself?

Bible Story (Acts 16:16-34)

Paul was a powerful preacher of Christ in the New Testament. He went with Silas to preach the Word of God to a place called Philippi. There he met with other brothers to pray. And every time they went, on the way, they met a girl who had an evil spirit who said to her: "These men are servants of the Most High God, who proclaim the way of salvation." And he did this every day. Until one day, Paul was moved by God and cast out the demon in the name of Jesus.

This girl was being used by her masters to make money (for the evil spirit in her told people things that no one knew, and people gave her money). So, when the men heard that the girl was free, they were very angry and punished Paul and Silas and threw them into prison. But in prison the servants of God prayed and sang to the Lord, and the Lord set them free. There was a great earthquake that miraculously opened the prison doors, and all the prisoners were set free. When the jailer saw that the prison doors had been opened, he thought that someone would kill him, so he drew his sword and was about to kill himself. But Paul cried out in a loud voice, saying, "Don't harm yourself, for we are all here."

Illustration

Randall Truman was a man who had a beautiful house at the foot of a mountain. The view was beautiful and Randall seemed to live very happily there. But suddenly, in 1980, that mountain —which was a volcanic mountain called St. Helen's in Washington State— began to smoke. The situation was clear: the volcano was going to erupt, and his beautiful house was right where the burning lava was going to flow.

Randall's family warned him of the danger, but he had no intention of leaving. Government agents also came to see him, but he refused to listen to them. Finally, the volcano erupted and Randall's house was buried under the burning lava and he died.

This illustrates that when someone harms his or her body, he or she is at risk of certain death. There are warnings, but if he or she does not get out of that (for example, drugs, or the vice of overeating), then sooner or later he or she will die. Randall thought that his home was the best place to live, but rather, it was the place of his death. As Christians, God commands us to take care of our body and treat it with respect because it is the temple of the Holy Spirit.

Questions About the Class

1. What are some ways a person can harm his body?
2. Why were Paul and Silas put in jail?
3. What did God do to free his servants? Why did the jailer want to kill himself?
4. What did Paul shout at the jailer?
5. What did his family and government agents warn Mr. Truman about?
6. What does the illustration teach us in this lesson?

Phrases to Memorize

1. God commands us to take care of our body because it is the temple of the Holy Spirit.
2. People who smoke, consume drugs or abuse food are showing that they do not take care of their own body and are heading for certain death if they do not get out of it.
3. Only Christ can free a person from addictions, but I must stay away from that, because even I, who have been washed with the blood of Jesus, could be caught by the devil if I allow it. I will not let myself be deceived by the devil!
4. The wise man sees evil coming and turns away. If I see a dangerous situation, I will turn away from it because God has ordered me to take good care of His temple, which is my body.

Other Bible passages on the theme for reading and memorization

2 Tim 1:7; 1 Cor. 6:19-20; 1 Pet. 5:7; Jn. 10:10; 1 Cor. 10:13; Lk. 1:37; Prov. 13:25; Prov. 25:16; Gal. 5:22-24; 1 Cor. 9:25-27; 2 Pet. 1:5-7.

24

Fidelity in Marriage

Memorize

Hebrews 13:4 "Give honor to marriage, and remain faithful to one another in marriage. God will surely judge people who are immoral and those who commit adultery."

<u>Adultery</u>: a married person goes to bed with someone other than the person who they are married to.

God created Adam first, and then Eve. This was the first marriage on earth. God did not create two women for Adam so that he could be married to both at the same time; or if he did not like the first one, he could then leave her and marry the other one, no. God created one man for one woman; and one woman for one man. One day you will most likely get married, and when that happens, God wants you to give your love only to that woman (if you are a man) or only to that man (if you are a woman). If a person who is married thinks of someone other than his wife or husband and desires in his heart to sleep with her/him, then he/she commits this terrible sin that is called adultery. This sin is horrible, because it destroys families.

❓ Introductory Questions

1. What does it mean to be faithful? How do people show that they are not faithful?
2. How do you show that you are a faithful person?
3. How does this topic have similarities with the topic of idolatry?

Bible Story (1 Samuel 2:12-26; 3:1-18)

The Old Testament law says that if a man or woman slept with someone other than their husband or wife, they were to be put to death. That's how serious that sin is in God's eyes.

There were many years ago, before Jesus was born, a priest of the Jewish nation named Eli. Eli had two sons (Hopni and Phinehas). What were their names? Eli did not raise his sons well, and they did evil in the eyes of God. They, being married, slept with women other than their wives, the same women who served in the place where God was worshiped. What Eli's sons did was very bad. What were their names?

God gave them a chance to repent, but they continued to do wrong. So, the Lord sent a prophet to tell Eli what He would do to his sons: they would be killed. Later, God used little Samuel to remind Eli what He would do to his sons.

Illustration

The Bible devotes many verses to warn against the sin of infidelity (adultery). Also, in the Book of Proverbs, God devotes almost three entire chapters to speak against this sin (chapters 5-7). One phrase within these chapters says: "But the man who commits adultery is an utter fool, for he destroys himself" (Prov. 6:32).

This means that the one who is unfaithful is a foolish person, because he/she corrupts his soul (causes his soul to spoil). Have you ever smelled something spoiled? For example, does a dead dog smell bad?

In 1971, a newspaper in Greece published a story about a man who was imprisoned for getting married twice within 48 hours. It turned out that he got married and went on his honeymoon with his wife to a certain city. However, on the trip, his car broke down and his wife returned to her place of residence by bus, while he stayed behind to repair the car. When that happened, he went to a bar and there he met another woman, and married her. He married her, and continued his honeymoon, but with a second woman!

❓ Questions About the Class

1. What does the Old Testament law say about someone who sleeps with someone who is not his or her husband?
2. What were Hophni and Phinehas doing?
3. What did God say to Eli regarding his children?
4. God used a child to remind Eli of what he would do with his children. What was that child's name?
5. What does a phrase from Proverbs (seen in class) say about someone who is unfaithful?
6. Why was a man imprisoned in Greece, according to the illustration?
7. Why is the sin of adultery so horrible to God? Because it destroys _____.

Phrases to Memorize

1. God wants you to marry a Christian boy or girl and be faithful to that person for the rest of your life.
2. God will punish people who do not obey him and do wrong, as in the case of Hophni and Phinehas.
3. For God, the sin of adultery is something very bad because it destroys families.
4. Whoever commits this sin makes his heart smell bad (like the smell of a dead dog).
5. Whoever does not want to fall into this sin must be careful about what he sees and what he thinks, because Jesus said that it is enough to want to sleep with someone who is not your husband (wife) to commit that sin in your heart.

Other Bible passages on the theme for reading and memorization

Mat. 5:27-28; Mal. 2:14; Eph. 5:33; Heb. 13:4; Exo. 20.14; 1 Cor. 6:18; Lev. 20:10; Dt. 22:22; 1 Cor. 6:9-10; Gal. 5:19; Mt. 15:19.

25

You Must Respect the Property of Others

Memorize

1 Corinthians 6:10 "not thieves nor the greedy nor drunkards not slanderers nor swindlers will inherit the kingdom of God."

There are many people who believe that stealing is okay. They say that if they steal from someone who has a lot, it is okay. Others say that they did not intend to do it, but they do not return what they accidentally took. Others think that it is okay because everyone or most people do it too. Others think that it is okay because they have a need to do it (for example, because they are hungry). Others think that it is okay to take what belongs to their friend (because they are friends) or worse, something belongs to their parents. Others think that if there is a lot of something, stealing just a little bit is not wrong. Others say that if someone stole from them, they have the right to do the same to him/her (or others). The Bible prohibits taking what is not ours.

? Introductory Questions

1. Have you ever known a boy or girl who takes what is not his/her?
2. What do you think will happen if you take what is not yours?
3. If someone takes what is not yours, what do you do?

Bible Story (2 Samuel 15:12-18:1-18)

Have you heard the story of Zacchaeus? Maybe you have heard it before, but I will tell it to you again. Zacchaeus was a tax collector. Taxes are money that the government collects from the people who live in the country. Well, Zacchaeus had the job of helping the Roman government (in Jesus' time) collect taxes. Zacchaeus had heard about Jesus and was very interested in seeing Him. But he had a problem, he was short and the crowd that followed Jesus prevented him from getting close to Him.

Then Zacchaeus had an idea, "I'll climb up a tree to see Jesus," he said to himself. When Zacchaeus climbed up the tree (a sycamore tree), he could see Jesus, but Jesus saw him too and said, "Hurry up, Zacchaeus, come down from there, for today I must stay at your house." So Zacchaeus climbed down from that tree and quickly went and opened the doors of his house to Jesus and his disciples. When Jesus was at Zacchaeus' house, Zacchaeus stood up and said, "if I have cheated people on their taxes, I will give them back four times as much."

Illustration

Eastern thieves are known for breaking into a house at the back and for being very clever thieves. It is said that on one occasion, many years ago, when India was ruled by the British, a British soldier was posted as the guard of his tent (for there were several soldiers living in this tent, and he had been left to look after their possessions). Well, while he was guarding the front, he did not notice that a thief had broken in at the back, dug a hole, got into the tent, and was taking everything out. The soldier had not noticed the thief and went into the tent to sleep, for it was already night and he was very sleepy. The thief was inside, but since it was dark, the soldier could not see him. When the soldier entered, the thief froze so as not to make any noise. As he froze, his arm was extended and his finger pointed at something; So, in the dark, the soldier wanted to put his helmet somewhere, and he thought that finger was a nail where he could hang his helmet. The thief stayed like that —paralyzed— until the soldier fell asleep, then he was able to leave with the loot, including the helmet. In the morning, everything that had happened was known.

Questions About the Class

1. What was Zacchaeus' problem in seeing Jesus? How did he solve it?
2. What did Jesus say to him when he saw him?
3. What did Zacchaeus say when Jesus and his disciples entered his house? Do you think a thief can ask for forgiveness and be forgiven by the Lord?
4. What are some excuses people often make for stealing?
5. How did the thief manage to rob the store that the British soldier was guarding?
6. What do you think the story of Zacchaeus teaches us?
7. Do thieves still get into heaven? Yes/no, why?

Phrases to Memorize

1. No matter what excuses or reasons a person gives for taking what is not his, stealing is still a sin before God.
2. He who has stolen something must return what is not his and ask for forgiveness.
3. Thieves will not enter heaven; therefore, it is very important to ask God for forgiveness and to ask for forgiveness from the one you have offended and make a deal with him to return all (or at least part) of what you have taken from him.
4. God forgives all who repent before Him and stop doing wrong.

Other Bible passages on the theme for reading and memorization

Eph. 4:28; Exo. 20:15; Mk. 10:19; Rom. 13:8-10; Rom. 13:9; Jas. 5:4; Heb. 13:5; Lev. 19:11; Mt. 19:18; Prov. 22:22; Hab. 2:6; Lk. 3:14; Tit. 2:10; 1 Ts. 4:6; Prov. 28;24; 1 Cor. 6:10.

26

Always Tell the Truth

Memorize

Ephesians 4:26 "Wherefore putting away lying, speak every man truth with his neighbour: for we are members one of another.

God commands all followers of Jesus to always tell the truth. Sometimes the truth seems to be against us, but this is only in appearance, because the truth will always be on our side. To be for the truth is to be for Christ Himself, because He is the truth (John 14:6).

? Introductory Questions

1. What are the benefits of always telling the truth?
2. What happens to someone who lie?
3. What could you do to get another person to tell the truth?

Bible Story (Acts 5:1-11)

After Jesus was resurrected and ascended into heaven, He sent the Holy Spirit and established His Church. The first church —the one in Jerusalem— was filled with the Holy Spirit, and God did great things. The sick was healed and many miracles happened. Those who were saved also received the gift of the Holy Spirit, spoke in tongues, met together often for communion, received teaching, and prayed together. Some of them owned property, and because they wanted to do good to those in need, they sold their property and brought the money to the apostles to distribute to the poor, widows, and orphans.

There was a married couple, his name was Ananias and her name was Sapphira. They sold a property, but instead of bringing all the money, they gave only a part and lied. They thought that no one would know, but God told Peter about this matter and he said to them, "You have not lied to men, but to God." And this sin was so serious that they both died that day.

Illustration

There was a man named Bob Harris who became famous as the weatherman. He studied geography and physics at three colleges, but failed to graduate from any of them. His dream was to get a job on television doing the weather; so he went to a prestigious television station in the US, and said he had a PhD in science from Columbia University in New York, but that was a lie. He got the job at that television station, and then another one, and then another one. So, by the age of 40, Bob was making a lot of money and fulfilling his dream.

Suddenly something happened. Someone wrote an anonymous letter to the television station, and the station investigated the man who called himself Dr. Bob. They discovered that what he had said about his studies was false, and this spread throughout the country. Bob Harris lost his job, and all the people who had previously welcomed him suddenly turned their backs on him. Fortunately, Bob apologized and a television station hired him.

Bob Harris had taken a shortcut, and made a mistake he would regret for the rest of his life.

Questions About the Class

1. What should you do when it seems that the truth is against you?
2. What was happening in the first church in Jerusalem?
3. What was done with the money that some people gave to the apostles when they sold their property?
4. What did Ananias and Sapphira do?
5. What happened to Ananias and Sapphira for doing what they did?
6. What was the serious mistake that Bob Harris made?
7. What are some of the problems that those who tell lies have to face? Do you think that liars always get caught? Yes/No, why?

Phrases to Memorize

1. When a person lies, he commits a sin before God.
2. The liar is then not believed by others.
3. Sooner or later the truth comes to light and the lie will be known.
4. God knows the hearts, and if no one notices a lie at that moment, the sin is there, because God does know.

Other Bible passages on the theme for reading and memorization

Prov. 6:16-19; Prov. 12:22; Prov. 19:9; Ps. 101:7; Prov. 12:19; Col. 3:9-10; Lk. 8:17; Jn. 8:44; Exo. 20:16; Eph. 4:25; 1 Jn. 2:4; Rev. 21:8; Lev. 19:11; Prov. 24.28; Prov. 14:5; Jn. 8:32.

27

Be Happy with What you Have Now

Memorize

Psalms 119:36 "Give me an eagerness for your laws rather than a love for money".

The word greed means to desire something eagerly. This includes material things, but it can also be other types of things that are not material. Can you name some of these things? For example, being popular or having prestige. This means that God wants you to be content with what He has given you and not desire what someone else has. This will make you pleasing to Him, and you will be happy.

? Introductory Questions

1. Can you mention the good things that God has given you?
2. Can you mention the good things that God has given to your brother or sister, your friend?
3. How does the good things that another person has make you happy?

Bible Story (Joshua 7:1-26)

The people of Israel had conquered Jericho and God ordered that no one should take what was in that city, because everything would be destroyed; and the gold and silver, bronze and iron that was there, would be consecrated to God.

Joshua then thought of the next city to conquer. This was a small city called Ai. He sent a small group of soldiers thinking it would be easy to conquer it, but instead, the men of Ai defeated them. Joshua did not know what was happening, and he prayed to God. So, the Lord told him that someone had taken the gold from the city, and that was the reason for their defeat. Joshua immediately went to investigate who had done this and realized that Achan was the person God was referring to. When he asked for an explanation, Achan confessed that he had seen and coveted that gold, and he had also taken other things. What happened next was very sad, because both he and his family were put to death.

Illustration

St. Augustine, a Christian writer who lived many centuries ago, wrote the following story in his book *Confessions*: "When I was a boy, I joined with another boy in trespassing on the property of a neighbor who had a pear tree. When we got there, we took as many as we could. Afterward, we ate several of them and threw the rest to the pigs. At home, I had much more delicious pears than these, but the ones I had coveted and taken seemed to me at the time to be the best, simply because they belonged to another person. I had the pleasure of having gone against the rules, and taking the forbidden fruit seemed to have made me happier at the time. But my greed made me a thief, and I suffered serious consequences later."

SPIRITUAL RESILIENCE

❓ Questions About the Class

1. What did God command the people of Israel not to take from Jericho?
2. What made Achan covet what he later took (even against God's command)?
3. What consequences did what he did have for Achan, for the people of Israel, for himself, and for his family?
4. Why did St. Augustine, as a child, trespass on someone else's property?
5. Why did St. Augustine think the coveted, and later stolen, pears were better than the ones he had at home? Were they really the best?
6. What gave St. Augustine pleasure? Does the pleasure of sin bring consequences? How serious are these consequences?
7. What should both Achan and St. Augustine have done to please God?

Phrases to Memorize

1. God wants you to be thankful and happy for what He has given you.
2. Every person has something that they can share with others and you should not desire what they have, but thank God for their life.
3. The sin of greed is the root of other sins, for example, the love of money.
4. God wants us to set our sights on Him and not on the things of this earth.

Other Bible passages on the theme for reading and memorization

Col. 3:5; Lk. 12:15; Heb. 13:5; Exo. 20:17; Eph. 5:5; Eph. 5:3; Lk. 12:15-21; 1 Jn. 2:15-17; 1 Tim. 6:10; Jer. 6:13; Jas. 4:2; Rom. 13:9; Ps. 119:36; Prov. 28:16.

Part IV. Christian Character

28

Judge not lest you be judged

Memorize

Matthew 7:1-2 "Judge not, that you be not judged. For with the judgment you pronounce you will be judged, and with the measure you use it will be measured to you."

Jesus forbids us to think badly of someone without first getting to know them, and we cannot think beyond the Acts and the proven behavior of someone. Suppose a new boy comes to class. The boy comes from a place where it is said that there are very aggressive people. In such a case, is it correct to say that the boy is aggressive only because he comes from there? That is judging. Also Jesus says that if you think badly of someone without getting to know them first, then the same will happen to you. The rule is this: you must think well of everyone and let them bear fruit (their works) then you will be able to see if they are good people or not; if they are Christians or not. Jesus said that their fruit will tell what they are like.

❓ Introductory Questions

1. If a person is doing something wrong, and you see it, for example, he has stolen something, and you tell him that he is a thief, is that judging him? (Talk to your dad/mom or instructor about this).
2. If you tell someone that what he says is contrary to the Bible, is that judging him? (Talk to your dad/mom or instructor about this).
3. If you tell someone that what he is doing is a sin, do you think you are judging him?

Bible Story (Acts 28:1-10)

To judge (as Jesus refers to in Mt. 7:1) is to think or say something that no one can know but God: what is in a person's heart and mind. We can only see actions and hear words; and sometimes, what we see and what we hear may not give us enough information. God wants our minds and hearts to be filled with truth, and if we don't have enough evidence of something, it is better to wait until we have it, and in the meantime, we should think well of people.

Paul, while traveling by ship to Rome, was shipwrecked. A shipwreck is the loss or sinking of a ship at sea. However, he and the others on the ship were saved by reaching an island called Malta. When they arrived, everyone was very cold, and they quickly went to get some branches to make a big fire. Paul also brought one, but he did not realize that the branch had a viper on it, and when he exposed it to the fire, the viper jumped and bit his hand. The bite of this type of viper was deadly, and the natives of the island, seeing this, thought that Paul must be a very bad man. They were judging Paul without having any proof. But later, he showed them that he was a powerful man of God, because he healed Publius' father in the name of Jesus. Publius was the most important person on the island.

Illustration

In his book *Illustrations of Bible Truth,* H.A. Ironside shares the following story. He tells of a certain Bishop Potter, who was traveling by ship to Europe from New York in the days before airplanes. Bishop Potter was to travel with another man in the same dressing room. He went, met his companion, and then went to the ship's office and said to the steward, "I wish this gold watch to be kept in the ship's safe. I hardly ever ask for such a thing, but this time the person I am traveling with seems to be a little unreliable." The steward replied, "Yes, Mr. Bishop; by the way, your companion came a few minutes ago and did exactly the same thing."

Questions About the Class

1. What does it mean to judge in Matthew 7:1?
2. What does God want our minds and hearts to be filled with? We are to think _____ about people.
3. What was the name of the island that Paul and those traveling with him landed on?
4. What did the Maltese people think of Paul? Why did they think that way?
5. How did Paul show them that their judgment was completely wrong?
6. Why did Bishop Potter want his watch kept for him?
7. What had Bishop Potter's companion done minutes before he arrived at the ship's office?

Phrases to Memorize

1. We should never think badly of people, because we do not know what is in their hearts.
2. We should wait for people to bear fruit (show words and deeds), because Jesus said, "By their fruits you will know them" (Mt. 7:16).
3. We should preach the Word of God (even if some say we are "judging" them), and if someone is doing wrong, we should say so.
4. If we think badly of other people, they will also think badly of us.
5. If someone has committed a sin, we should love them anyway and help them so that they do not do wrong anymore.

Other Bible passages on the theme for reading and memorization

Mt. 7:1-5; Lk. 6:37-42; Jn. 7:24; Jas. 4:11-12; Jas. 4:12; Rom. 2:1-3; Eph. 4:29; Rom. 14:4; Gal. 6:1.

29

We are the Salt of the Earth And the Light of the World

Memorize

Matthew 5:13 "You are the salt of the earth, but if salt has lost its taste, how shall its saltiness be restored? It is no longer good for anything except to be thrown out and trampled under people's feet."

Being a Christian means being a follower of Jesus, and as followers of Jesus we are the salt of the earth. Can you tell me why we put salt on our food? I know; you said it makes it taste better, and that's true. But also—perhaps you didn't know this— salt helps food not to spoil. This means that Christians, with our behavior and words, give flavor to the world and prevent it from spoiling. Likewise, Jesus has said that Christians are the light of the world.

❓ Introductory Questions

1. Can you tell us a story about a good deed that you or a Christian you know has done recently?
2. Why do you think it is so important for a Christian to do good deeds?
3. Do you think that if you do good deeds you will get into heaven?

Bible Story (Acts 16:14)

The Bible says very clearly that good works do not open the doors of heaven, but faith in Jesus does (read Ephesians 2:8-9 again. Yet, what sets apart the ones who have been born again is their good works. Good works are the result of faith in Jesus, and the power of the Holy Spirit in us. He is the one who does those good works through us. No one who calls himself a Christian can stop doing good works, because Jesus said that good works are the fruit of a Christian.

Paul was sent to preach the gospel to Philippi. When Paul arrived there (he was with other Christians) he began to preach the gospel on the riverbank, and a woman named Lydia, who was a textile seller, listened very carefully to what Paul said and believed the Word of God. When Lydia believed in the Lord Jesus — because Paul told her about Him— she was saved. So, do you know what she did right away? She begged Paul and his companions to stay at her house. Paul and the others would no longer have to pay for lodging or food. Lydia, that woman who had believed in the Lord Jesus, was willing to help them. That is the fruit that God expects from all of us, and the fruit (good works) confirms that we have believed in Jesus. Lydia was beginning to be the salt of the earth and the light of the world.

Illustration

During the Russian-Ukrainian war, in which Russia invaded part of Ukrainian territory, millions of people had to flee the country. Most of these people were women and children, as men were called up by the Ukrainian government to fight for their country. Among these women who fled were those who had very young children, and some even carried their babies in their arms.

The country that was receiving the most of these people – who are called refugees – was Poland. And it was quite touching to see that at one of the train stations in Poland (where the Ukrainian refugees were arriving), there were a good number of baby strollers waiting: a group of Polish Christian women had had this idea and had bought these strollers for the Ukrainian babies. Inside the strollers there were also baby bottles and bottle warmers and other essential items. Do you also want to do good deeds? These Polish Christian women were being the salt of the earth and the light of the world.

Also, Jesus said that if the salt loses its flavor (fades away), it is no longer good for anything. This means that Christians should keep doing good works throughout their lives.

❓ Questions About the Class

1. Where did Paul and his friends go to preach?
2. Who was Lydia?
3. Why do I say in the Bible Story that Lydia began to be the salt of the earth and the light of the world?
4. Why does Jesus say that Christians are the salt of the earth and the light of the world? What does salt do? What are the benefits of light?
5. Why can Christians do more and better good works than those who do not know God?
6. What was the good work that the Polish Christian women did?
7. What happens if salt stops having flavor? What does that mean?

Phrases to Memorize

1. None of us will get into heaven by doing good works, but true Christians keep doing good works.
2. The sign that a person has been saved is that he does the good works that he could not do before he was born again.
3. Christians can do good works (better than those who do not know God) because of the power of the Holy Spirit in them (in us).
4. If a Christian stops doing good works, then he becomes a tasteless salt and Jesus said that salt is good for nothing, but to be trampled underfoot by people.

Other Bible passages on the theme for reading and memorization

Mt. 5:16; Acts. 9:36; Acts. 10: 1-4; Eph. 2:10; 1 Ti. 5:25; 1 Ti. 6:18; Tit. 2:7; Tit. 2.14; Tit. 3:8, 14; Heb. 10:24; 1 Pet. 2:12.

30

See no One Unclothed

Memorize

Exodus 20:26 "And you shall not go up by steps to my altar, that your nakedness be not exposed on it".

When Adam and Eve were in the Garden of Eden they were naked (without clothes) because they had no sin. So, two babies who are without clothes do not think of doing anything wrong: they are innocent. But, the Bible says that after Adam and Eve sinned, they tried to cover themselves, and then God himself covered them. Since then, God wants all human beings to have clothes and not have their body uncovered. You, from now on that you are a boy (girl) must learn that God does not want you to see anyone without clothes nor to show your body without clothes. You must think that you will not see anyone without clothes until you get married, and then you will be able to see your husband (wife) like that, because for God those who are spouses are like one person.

? Introductory Questions

1. Have you ever heard any of your schoolmates talk about seeing someone without clothes? (You should immediately stay away from such people).
2. What kind of videos/photos are popular among your schoolmates to watch??
3. Are you curious about seeing another person without clothes?

Bible Story (Genesis 9:18-18)

Some people are curious to see another person without clothes, but that is a trap of the devil. You must understand that this is a very bad thing. The only person God wants you to see without clothes (outside yourself, of course) is your husband (wife), that is, when you get married, and that will be the only person God wants you to see like that throughout your life. Likewise, showing your body without clothes is the highest level of intimacy, that is, your naked body is the most personal thing you have, and only your husband (wife) will have the privilege to see it.

The Bible says that Noah drank too much grape juice and got drunk. You have to be very careful not to drink anything that has alcohol in it, because people who get drunk do things that bring them much sadness later in life. So, when he got drunk, he took off his clothes. And his younger son, Ham, found it interesting to see his father without clothes, and he made fun of him. This was a very serious sin, because afterward he was cursed all the days of his life, that is, he did not do well for the rest of his life.

Illustration

Snake charmers originated in Egypt, and although this "charming" is false (because the snake cannot hear the flute or pungi), this was for a long time the way some people made a living.

One of these charmers went into the forest, caught a snake, and put it in a basket. In the charmer's house lived a little mouse with his mother. The little mouse was very curious and liked to get into places where he shouldn't. His mother had warned him many times that his curiosity could get him into serious trouble, but he didn't listen. When the charmer put the basket inside the house, the little mouse saw it and was curious to see what was inside. "Maybe there are some tasty candies in it that I can eat until I'm full," he thought. So, he tried to see what was inside, but it was impossible. Then he tried to open the basket, but that still couldn't happen. Finally, he came up with the idea of making a hole in the basket with his sharp teeth, so he started biting and biting until he made a hole big enough to get into. The snake was inside, and waited patiently, and immediately the little mouse came in, boom! He swallowed it in one bite. Then the snake went out through the hole and returned to the forest.

This story illustrates to us that we should not be curious about what is behind each person's clothes, because this will be like a snake that will bite us immediately.

Questions About the Class

1. Who is the only person you should ever see without clothes on in your life (other than yourself)?
2. Why is your spouse the only person you should ever show your naked body to?
3. What was the grave sin that Ham committed?
4. What happened to Ham for committing that sin?
5. Can snakes really be charmed by "snake charmers"?
6. What happened to the little mouse in the story? Why did that happen to him?
7. What does the story of the illustration teach us?

Phrases to Memorize

1. We must be very careful not to see anyone without clothes, it is better to close our eyes and leave that place, because this will avoid serious problems in life.
2. One day you will see a person without clothes, and this will be your husband or wife. Then everything will be fine with that, for now it is a sin.
3. When a person sees someone without clothes for the first time, then this will be like having taken a drug, because the human being wants to continue sinning
4. Sin brings a little pleasure, but later it brings great destruction.
5. You must not be curious to get into a place from which you will not be able to get out without suffering harm.
6. The Bible warns a lot to stay away from this type of sin, because it is very destructive.

Other Bible passages on the theme for reading and memorization

Hab. 2:15; 1 Cor. 6:9, 13, 18; 1 Pet. 2:11; 2 Ti. 2:22; Col. 3:5; Eph. 5:3; 1 Jn. 2:16; Gal. 5:19; Heb. 13:4; Job 31:1; Mt. 5:28; Ps. 119:37; Jas. 1:14-15.

31

Fasting

Memorize

Luke 4:1-2 "And Jesus, full of the Holy Spirit, returned from the Jordan and was led by the Spirit in the wilderness for forty days, being tempted by the devil. And he ate nothing during those days. And when they were ended, he was hungry."

We all love food. What is your favorite food? Do you like chocolates, cakes, and cookies? Yes! Most of us like those things, but did you know that Christians should also fast? You don't know what fasting is, right? Fasting is stopping eating food and only drinking water. In the Bible, both in the Old and New Testament, all men and women of God fasted. Jesus and the apostles also fasted; however, children and teenagers do not fast (because they are growing). Phew! You're saved by the bell! But, it is important for you to know that one day, when you are about 18 years old, you will be able to start fasting a full day without food. No way, you will have to wait! Oh! But the good news is that you can start training yourself to fast by having days without sweets or desserts.

❓ Introductory Questions

1. Do you know what fasting is for?
2. Did you know that fasting is good for adults?
3. Do you eat snacks? What kind of snacks do you eat?

Bible Story (Luke 4:1-10)

Fasting is necessary for all adult Christians because it is a discipline that helps us focus on the Lord and pray better. Fasting is always combined with prayer; for it is useless to fast without praying. You can also spend a good amount of time reading the Bible. In the Bible, we can see that men and women of God fasted regularly (in private); and in public in times of crisis. It is also a dedication of your body to the Lord, because with it, you say that God is more important than food. With fasting, you show that your search for God is serious.

The most important example of fasting is our Lord Jesus. He fasted, do you know how many days? Exactly! He fasted for 40 days! And during this time, He was in the desert, praying to God. Moses fasted for 40 days, and he was on top of Mount Sinai, praying to the Lord, and so was Elijah. The Lord Jesus was filled with the Holy Spirit and the Holy Spirit led Him into the desert to fast and pray; and when He was there, He had to fight against the devil, but He won.

Illustration

You may have seen a basketball game before. Basketball is a very fast game; points are scored very quickly. Unlike soccer, in basketball two minutes can mean an eternity, and the team that is leading can lose the game in the last seconds. A single long-distance three-point shot taken at the last second can decide the game. The last seconds of a basketball game are often the most exciting.

The devil, in the temptation of Jesus, came to Him to tempt Him, just when He was finishing His fast, on the 40th day. The devil wanted to ruin everything, precisely at the last moment: the Lord Jesus was very hungry, tired and alone. However, He, although He was physically weak, was very strong spiritually. Thus, the devil will be able to attack you in the last moments before finishing your fast, and he will want to make you fall, but you will win, as Jesus won.

Questions About the Class

1. Since children and adolescents do not fast (because they are growing), what can you do to practice fasting and dedicate this to God?
2. What is the most important practice of fasting?
3. What is the purpose of fasting?
4. How many days did Jesus fast? On which of those days was he attacked by the devil?
5. Apart from the Lord Jesus Christ, what other servants of God also fasted for 40 days?
6. Should we pay special attention to the end of our fast? Why?
7. What does the basketball game in the illustration teach us?

Phrases to Memorize

1. Fasting is a Christian discipline that needs to be practiced often.
2. Children and teenagers do not fast, but they can start practicing by not eating sweets and desserts for a whole day.
3. Fasting is a private practice, but there are also times when a group can fast (a church, for example).
4. Fasting helps us focus on God and pray better. Also, during the time of fasting, we can spend more time reading the Bible than usual.
5. It is not a requirement that all Christians fast for 40 days (like Jesus), and the Bible does not say how often you should fast, but you should make sure that you do it from time to time.
6. Fasting will help you improve your relationship with God, and it will give you much joy, because what we Christians seek on this earth is to be as close as possible to our Lord Jesus.

Other Bible passages on the theme for reading and memorization

Mt. 6:16-18; Jl. 2:12; Is.58:3-7; Ps. 69:10; Dn. 10:3; Acts. 14:23; Esd. 8:23; Neh. 1:4; Lk. 4:2; Acts. 13:2-3; Ps. 35:13; Mt. 4:4; Est. 4:16; Lk. 2:37; Exo. 34:28; 2 S. 1:12; 1 Cor. 10:31.

32

True Wealth

Memorize

Luke 12:15 "Take care, and be on your guard against all covetousness, for one's life does not consist in the abundance of his possessions."

The world we live in today will teach you that your goal should be to be rich. If you ask your classmates at school who wants to be rich, they will all raise their hands. However, Jesus said that this is not the meaning of life. Jesus wants you and I to understand that following Him and being with Him is the most wonderful thing we can have in this life; and to be with Him you need to love Him. How can you be sure that you love Jesus? Yes! If you obey what He says.

❓ Introductory Questions

1. What do you want to be when you grow up?
2. Not everyone will be rich, what do you think is the reason?
3. Do you think there are better things than money? What are these things?

Bible Story (2 Chronicles 9:13-29; Ecclesiastes 12:13)

In the passage you just read, the one from 2 Chronicles, speaks of the wealth and fame that King Solomon achieved. Solomon was the son of King David, and God prospered him financially. He had a lot of gold and silver, including a collection of shields made of pure gold. He sat on a large throne made of ivory. Do you know what ivory is? Ivory is the material from elephant tusks. There was no throne like Solomon's among all the kings of his time.

The king had ships that brought gold, silver, ivory, and also monkeys and peacocks. He also had an abundance of clothing, thousands of horses. Do you have a horse? Are horses expensive? His houses and palaces were also made of very expensive materials and the best wood.

Solomon was very intelligent and knew many things, but if you read the Book of Ecclesiastes, you will realize that he was not happy with everything he had. And at the end of his life, he said that only one thing is necessary: to fear God and obey his commandments, that is the meaning of life.

Illustration

Have you heard who Albert Einstein was? Albert Einstein was a very famous scientist because of the great discoveries he made. One day Albert was on a train in Germany and the train inspector was marking the passengers' tickets. When he arrived with Albert Einstein and asked for his ticket, he got nervous and started searching in all his pockets, but he couldn't find the ticket. The inspector recognized him and exclaimed: "Oh, but you are the famous Albert Einstein! No, you don't have to show me any ticket, I know who you are, and

I know that you would never travel on the train without paying." The inspector left and continued with his work. Later, when he came back, Albert continued searching, now under the seat. So, the inspector said to him: "Mr. Einstein, don't worry, please, I know who you are!" said the inspector. "Yes, I know that you know who I am," said Albert finally, "the problem is that I don't know where I am going."

This story teaches us that a person can have a lot of money and a lot of fame, but he may not know where he is going. Are you sure that you are going to heaven? All those who have faith in Jesus and have made Him Lord and Savior go to heaven. That is what really matters in life.

Questions About the Class

1. What does the world teach you should be your goal?
2. What does Jesus say is not life?
3. How rich was Solomon? Can you tell me some things that Solomon had?
4. What did Solomon say at the end of his life?
5. Why did Albert Einstein want to find his ticket?
6. What does the illustration's story teach us?

Phrases to Memorize

1. As a Christian, your goal in life should not be to be rich or famous. Your goal should be to follow Jesus to the end.
2. Solomon was not happy being so rich and famous, and he said that what really matters in life is to obey God's commandments.
3. True wealth consists in Jesus being your friend, being with Him and Him with you, obeying Him in everything and being like Him.
4. The most important thing is to always be sure that you are going to heaven and to keep your faith in Jesus all your life.
5. Not all the kids who want to be rich today will be, but if God wants you to be rich, you must use your money to help the poor and for the Word of God to be preached.

Other Bible passages on the theme for reading and memorization

Heb 13:5; Mt. 6:24; Mal. 3:10; Prov. 13:22; Dt. 8:18; 1 Ti. 6:10; 1 Ti. 5:8; Lk. 12:14; Prov. 10:22; 2 Cor. 8:9; Prov. 28:20; Prov. 22:7; Prov. 13:11; Mt. 25:14-30.

33

Help the Poor

Memorize

Psalms 41:1 "Blessed is he that considereth the poor: the LORD will deliver him in time of trouble".

You may have seen a homeless person before. A homeless person is considered an outcast, and an outcast is a person that no one wants to associate with because people consider him inferior. These people are out on the streets and they don't have a home to live in, they are poor. But there are also poor people who have a home, and being poor in the United States is not the same as being poor in India or Somalia (Africa). So, a poor person is someone who has less than us. God has commanded that Christians always give to the poor.

Introductory Questions

1. What is a poor person for you?
2. Why do you think a person is poor?
3. How could you help the poor?

Bible Story (Ruth 1:1-23)

You should never judge others, remember? Many times, we don't know why a poor person is in that condition. People can speak badly of them, but we should never do so. The Bible speaks of Ruth and Naomi. They were very poor, but it was because they were widowed.

The Book of Ruth actually tells us the story of three widows. All three had Jewish husbands; the mother and her two sons. It all started when Naomi, her husband and their two sons moved to Moab, a country neighboring Israel. But in Moab, Naomi's husband died, and her sons married Moabite women. Then her sons also died; so, Naomi decided to return to her land. Then she told her daughters-in-law that they could do whatever they wanted. One of them decided to stay and the other (Ruth) wanted to go with Naomi.

When they were in Bethlehem in the land of Judah, Naomi and Ruth were so poor that they had nothing to eat. So, Ruth, who was very young, went to the fields of a man named Boaz. God's law said that after the reapers had gathered the wheat, they were not to go back to gather what had fallen, because that was for the poor. Boaz, the owner of the field, not only let Ruth gather the wheat that had been left behind, but he also gave her food and water. He also treated Ruth with courtesy and respect.

Illustration

An Australian Franciscan friar was very excited when he was assigned to be Mother Teresa's guide and assistant on her trip to New South Wales (Australia). He always dreamed of being close to such a great person to learn from her, and then tell his friends.

However, the days passed, and although he was very close to Mother Teresa, he never had the opportunity to talk to her, because she was always surrounded by people. Finally, the day came for her to leave, and her next destination would be New Guinea (another island that is 4 hours away by plane). So, frustrated and desperate, the friar said to Mother Teresa: "If I pay for my plane ticket to New Guinea, can I sit next to you so we can talk, and you can teach me how much you know?" Then she answered him with a question: "Do you have enough money to pay for your plane ticket to New Guinea?" "Yes!" she replied enthusiastically. "Well, then give that money to the poor. If you do, you will have learned much more than I can teach you."

❓ Questions About the Class

1. Do you know people who are poorer than you? Is it a choice or an order from God that we give to the poor? Why should we not judge the poor?
2. What did God command to be done when the wheat was harvested from the fields?
3. What acts of generosity did Boaz do with Ruth?
4. Why were Ruth and Naomi so poor?
5. What was the illusion that the Franciscan friar had when he was close to Mother Teresa?
6. What did she answer when the friar told her that he had the money to pay for his plane ticket to New Guinea?

Phrases to Memorize

1. In both, the Old and New Testament, God commands us to care for and help the poor.
2. We should not think badly of the poor, because we do not know the true causes of their situation, we should only help them.
3. There will always be people poorer than us, and God will always give us opportunities to help them.
4. God will bless all those who have compassion for the poor. You should practice giving. God wants you to give, even if it is not as much as others give.
5. Not only give money, but you can also give your things to the poor. And when you do, give the best and do not feel that you are better or more important than them, because they are just like you.

Other Bible passages on the theme for reading and memorization

Job 31:16; Job 29:12; Jer. 22:16; Prov. 19:17; Ps. 41:1; Acts. 9:36; Mt. 6:3; Job 29:16; Dt. 15:11; Prov. 21:13; Dt. 15:7; Is. 58:7; Ps. 9:18; Gal. 2:10.

34

Do Not Be Angry

Memorize

Psalms 37:8 "Stop being angry! Turn from your rage! Do not lose your temper —it only leads to harm.

The Christian should almost always be a calm and peaceful person who rarely gets angry. Jesus was angry four times: (1) When a religious practice was put before human need (Mark 3:4-5); (2) When children were not allowed to come to Him (Mark 10:13-14); (3) When material gains were an obstacle for people to pray (Mt. 21:12-13); and, (4) When His disciples did not have the faith to free a demoniac (Mt. 17:17). But, He never got angry because He had been offended, neither because of pride, much less because of envy, nor because of all those sins that usually make human beings angry. Jesus never sinned.

? Introductory Questions

1. How often do you get angry?
2. What causes you to get angry?
3. How do you react when someone gets angry with you?

Bible Story (Numbers 20:1-10)

Many people have done crazy things when they were angry, and their crazy actions have brought them great trouble. Getting angry itself is not what is wrong, but the reasons why someone gets angry, and the length of time they stay angry. We have the example of Jesus, He got angry very few times, and it was always for the right reasons; He never let his anger lead him to think of doing something wrong. This was not the case with Moses.

Moses was the meekest person on earth (are you like that too?) and he put up with the people of Israel many times. But there was one occasion when the people became angry with him again. They spoke very rudely to him, and complained about him having brought them out of Egypt; this time it was because they had no water. Moses then went to God and asked for instructions to solve the situation. God told him to take his staff and speak to the Rock that always walked with them (1 Cor. 10:4). But Moses, instead of speaking to the Rock, got angry, spoke harshly to the people, and struck the Rock twice. Then God punished him for having disobeyed Him, and told him that he would not enter the promised land either.

Illustration

In 1992, Our Daily Bread devotional published an account of something that happened in 1894. The Baltimore Orioles went to play an ordinary game in Boston. But what happened that day was something extraordinary. John McGraw happened to get into an argument with the Boston team's third baseman, and soon they were fighting. The rest of the players also got involved in the fight, and then the spectators. One of them started a fire, and the stadium burned to the ground. But that wasn't all. The fire spread to other buildings nearby, and 107 buildings burned down as well.

In James 3:5 we read, "Behold, how great a forest a little fire kindles!" Your anger could be so damaging that not only you but others will be affected.

Questions About the Class

1. Why is it important to never get angry?
2. In what unique circumstances did the Lord Jesus get angry?
3. If you do get angry one day, what should you always avoid? Why is it very important to control your emotions?
4. Why did Moses get angry?
5. What were the consequences of Moses' anger?
6. Why did a stadium and 107 buildings burn down in Boston in 1894?

Phrases to Memorize

1. The character of Christ in us is one of gentleness and never anger.
2. There are few occasions in our lives when we should get angry (for Jesus' reasons), but we should always control our feelings and not sin.
3. When a person gets angry and fights with others, there will always be negative consequences.
4. When someone speaks to us aggressively, we should respond with kindness.
5. If you let yourself be carried away by anger, this will be like a river that takes you into a whirlpool from which it will be difficult to get out.

Other Bible passages on the theme for reading and memorization

Prov. 14:29; Ps. 37:8; Prov. 15:1, 18; Jas. 1:19-20; Eph. 4:26; Ecc.7:9; Prov. 29:11; Prov. 19:11; Eph. 4:31; Prov. 16:32; Col 3:8; Mt. 5:22; Ps. 103:8.

35

Missionaries

Memorize

Romans 10:15 "And how shall they preach, except they be sent? As it is written, How beautiful are the feet of them that preach the gospel of peace, and bring glad tidings of good things!"

A missionary is a person who is sent to another country or culture in order to preach the good news of salvation and establish new churches. We see the first missionaries in the Book of Acts. Paul and Barnabas were the first Christian missionaries; however, in the Old Testament there are some people mentioned who were—in some way—missionaries as well.

❓ Introductory Questions

1. What does a missionary do?
2. Do you know any missionaries? What are their names? Where do they serve?
3. Why do you think the work of missionaries is important?

Bible Story (2 Kings 5:1-5)

In the days of the prophet Elisha, certain soldiers from the country of Syria had taken a girl captive, who had ended up in the house of a general of the army of Syria named Naaman.

Naaman was a very brave person, but he had leprosy. Leprosy is a skin disease that, in Bible times, was incurable. So, this girl who served in Naaman's house preached to the God of Israel and recommended that he seek out the prophet Elisha, who was used by God to heal the sick. The story goes on to say that Naaman went to seek out the prophet Elisha, but he was not healed in the way he wanted. So, does this girl fit the description of a missionary? What is missing? Why do you think so?

Illustration

The first evangelical missionary of modern times was William Carey (1761-1834); he was a missionary in India. God called him to do missions in India at a time when the churches were not sending missionaries anywhere. He was born in Northamptonshire, England and worked as a shoemaker, but while working as a shoemaker he also served as a pastor in the town where he was born.

However, William Carey was called by God to preach Jesus Christ in India. He founded the English Baptist Missionary Society in 1792. And in India he was called "the father of Bengali prose" because he managed to write several grammar books and dictionaries of that language. Carey also learned other Indian languages (besides Bengali): Marathi, Oriya, Hindi, Marathi, Assamese and Sanskrit, and he translated the Bible into all these languages. His influence was powerful in causing the Indian government to prohibit the murder of children and to prevent the killing of the wives of Indians who died (these things were traditions of the Indian religion, Hinduism).

You can read the very interesting biographies of the following missionaries: Adoniram Judson (1788-1850) and Ann Judson (1789-1829); George Müller (1805-1898), David Livingstone (1813-1873), Mary Slessor (1848-1915), J. Hudson Taylor (1932-1905), Amy Carmichael (1867-1951), John Stam (1907-1934) and Elisabeth "Betty" Stam (1906-1934), Elisabet Elliot (1926-2015), Helen Roseveare (1925-2016), among many others.

❓ Questions About the Class

1. Who were the first Christian missionaries?
2. What did the girl who served in Naaman's house do?
3. Who is considered the first evangelical missionary of modern times?
4. What did William Carey do in India?
5. What other names of missionaries can you mention?
6. Are you interested in reading their biographies?

Phrases to Memorize

1. Missionaries have a very important job, because they take the gospel to places where there are no Christian churches yet.
2. The most important functions of a missionary are to preach the gospel and establish churches. But they can also write books and spread the gospel through written form.
3. Missionaries are people who dedicate their lives to the service of the Lord, therefore, you should have great respect and admiration for all of them.
4. They need to be supported by the churches, therefore, you should propose in your heart to give everything you can for missionary work. You should also pray for them every day.

When you give, you should do it for God and not so that people can see what you give.

Other Bible passages on the theme for reading and memorization

Mr. 16:15; Mt. 28:19-20; Acts. 6:4; Acts. 1:8; Ps. 96:3; Rom. 10:14; 1 Pet. 3:15; Is. 6:8; Mt. 24:14; Jn. 3:16; Lk. 18:29-30; Is. 49:6; Is. 52:7; Gn. 12:1.

36

Be Grateful

Memorize

1 Thessalonians 5:18 "In everything give thanks: for this is the will of God in Christ Jesus concerning you."

Gratitude sees each day as a gift. Grateful people are more focused on what they have received and the privileges they have than on what they lack. Gratitude is what leads us to praise God's greatness and worship. We can say that the reason God gives us so many gifts is so that we can recognize them and worship Him. If we are not grateful, then we begin to think that what we have is because we have gotten it by ourselves, and it was not God. This is an act of rebellion against Him. We should not assume that we deserve something or that we have it because we must have it; everything we have is because God has given it to us and it is for His glory.

Introductory Questions

1. Think about what you have, can you mention some of these things?
2. What things do you have that others don't have?
3. What makes you deserve these things that you have?
4. What makes you feel most grateful to God?

Bible Story (Numbers 13:1-14:19)

An ungrateful person is one who forgets or fails to show gratitude for the kindness he/she has received. He is unable to understand the gifts and benefits he has received and now enjoys.

The people of Israel were blessed by God. They were a nation of slaves, slaves who worked all day carrying heavy bricks; without rest (they did not have a day of rest); without medical services; without pay; living in misery, etc. Nevertheless, God gave them freedom: now they enjoyed the protection of the Lord and had everything. They had God himself as a doctor, since they had no hospitals or doctors in the desert; they had free food every day; a cloud gave them shade during the day and a pillar of fire warmed them during the night. They did not have to work at heavy tasks, etc. And now, God made them be on the border of the promised land. A land flowing with milk and honey.

They sent out 12 spies, but do you know what happened? Exactly! They grumbled against God and thought badly of Him. They were so ungrateful that they said, "I wish we had died in the land of Egypt; or in this wilderness, I wish we had died!" (v. 2). They soon forgot what God had done for them, and they did not believe in His goodness.

Illustration

Did you know that there are millions of reasons to be thankful to God? It is very important to always be thankful because this makes you find reasons to worship God. Jeremiah 15:19 says: "Therefore thus says the LORD: If you return, I will restore you, and you shall stand before Me; and if you select the precious from the vile, you shall be as My mouth. Let them return to you, but you shall not return to them." The grateful heart always finds reasons to thank God, and to select the good from all circumstances.

At the time you are taking this lesson, there are many things going on in your body that you are not able to see or understand yourself. For example, did you know that your heart will beat perhaps 3 billion times during your lifetime? And what about your brain! The brain has about 100 billion cells, and all those cells work! It's like 100 billion mini-computers working together! Do you know what a cell in your body is? Your brain will continue to grow until you are 18 years old, and although it only weighs 2% of your body, it uses 20% of all your energy.

Did you know that the human eye can distinguish at least 1 million different colors? There are so many amazing facts about how the human body works. Can you research some more on Google? (type: "wonders of the human body" in the search engine).

❓ Questions About the Class

1. What are some characteristics of people who are thankful?
2. Why is it so important to be thankful to God?
3. What happens if you are not thankful to God?
4. Can you define what an ungrateful person is?
5. What did the Israelites not have that later God gave them when He delivered from Egypt? What were the problems they used to have in Egypt? Did they continue having them after God freed them?
6. What did the ungrateful Israelites say?
7. Can you mention some of the wonders of your body? (All of this is given by God).

Phrases to Memorize

1. Every day when you wake up, the first thing you should think about is what God has given you and the reasons you have to be thankful; then you should tell Him this in prayer.
2. You should focus on what you have received from God and what you have now, not on what you do not have.
3. You should always think about the positive things you are enjoying, because everything good is created by God. Then you will speak like God (Jer. 15:19).
4. At night, before you go to sleep, think about the good things you received from the Lord during the day, and tell them to God in prayer.

Other Bible passages on the theme for reading and memorization

1 Ts. 5:18; Ps. 107:1; Eph. 5:20; Col. 3:15-17; Jas. 1:17; Fil. 4:6; 2 Cor. 9:15; Ps. 106:1; Ps. 105:1; Col. 3:15; Ps. 100:4; Col. 4:2; Ps. 20:4; Ps. 30:12; Rom. 1:21; Ps. 95:2; Phm. 1:4.

37

Fear of God

Memorize

Psalms 25:14 "The Lord confides in those who fear him; he makes his covenant known to them."

In this verse you have memorized it says that God makes friends with those who fear Him. There are many aspects to this important topic, and here I will be talking about some of the most important ones. Every human being has fear in one way or another, but that feeling should be directed toward God and Him alone. Jesus said not to fear those who kill the body but to fear God, who can not only kill the body, but also condemn us eternally (read Mt. 10:28). Only if we manage to understand and practice the fear of God will we be able to be free from the fear of the devil and the fear of everything that is not God.

❓ Introductory Questions

1. Do you think that God, being loving, can get angry?
2. How would you react if you saw an injustice before your eyes (for example, an older child hitting a younger one)? Have you ever seen something like that?
3. How would you react if the earth suddenly opened up? (Num. 16:1-32).
4. What would you think of God if you knew that He killed two people who lied to the Holy Spirit?

Bible Story (Acts 5:1-11)

The fear of God teaches us that God is not only love, mercy, and forgiveness, but He is also holy, just, and righteous. The fear of God helps us understand what God is like (according to the Scriptures). The fear of God makes us stand in awe of how great He is, and thus give great reverence to the Lord. It also makes our hearts beat faster, because we know that what He says is always true, and we have to give an account of our actions, both here and on the day of judgment. The Bible says that one definition of the fear of God is to hate evil, arrogance, and the wrong way (Prov. 8:13); therefore, everyone who fears God turns away from sin, because he knows that sin produces destruction and death. And God is no respecter of persons (Eph. 6:9; Col. 3:25; 1 Pet. 1:17).

The case of Ananias and Sapphira (which I already mentioned in another class) helps us to better understand what the fear of God means. Ananias and Sapphira sinned before God, they lied to the Holy Spirit and suffered a terrible punishment for it. If you or I had been there and had seen everything that happened, I am sure that we would stay away from all sin as far as possible. The fear of God always goes hand in hand with the love of God and you cannot have one without having the other. Can you tell the story of Ananias and Sapphira yourself? Do you remember it?

Illustration

One of the best illustrations of the fear of God is the relationship between a father and his son. A father who loves his son also disciplines him, because he knows that if he does not discipline him, then sooner or later that son can become a delinquent. Discipline is a demonstration of the father's love. The child knows that when dad is talking seriously, he has to pay attention. Do you have a father like that? If you do, thank God, because your dad loves you. The child who is disciplined when he does something wrong, knows that his dad loves him.

On the other hand, the child who says to his father, "I am not afraid of you," is showing that he does not love him. There is also a kind of fear that is not good: being afraid that my father will not keep his promises or that he will cause me harm. That is not the kind of fear that God commands us to have of Him, for that "fear of God" is a false fear of God. For the true fear of God means having complete trust in Him and loving Him with all our heart at the same time, for we know that He always desires our good; He is infinitely good.

❓ Questions About the Class

1. The fear of God teaches us that He is not only love, mercy, and forgiveness but He is also _____, _____, and _____.
2. The fear of God is also a great _____.
3. What is the definition that the Bible gives us of the fear of God?
4. What did Jesus tell us about the fear of God? (Read Matthew 10:28 and Luke 12:5)
5. What does the case of Ananias and Sapphira teach us about the fear of God?
6. How can we illustrate the fear of God with the relationship of a godly and good Christian father with his son?
7. What is a false fear of God?

Phrases to Memorize

1. The fear of God is always linked to the love of God and one cannot exist without the other.
2. Jesus taught us to fear God and not to fear anything or anyone else.
3. The fear of God frees us from all other fears.
4. The fear of God is to hate all evil and to obey the Lord with all our heart.
5. The Christian who fears God knows that God is serious and always tells the truth, so he takes into account his warnings as well as his promises of good.

Other Bible passages on the theme for reading and memorization

Prov. 1:7; Prov. 8:13; Job 28:28; Mt. 10:28; Ps. 111:10; Ecc. 12:13; Ps. 33:8; Lk. 1:50; Prov. 14:27; Dt. 10:12; 1 Jn. 4:18; Prov. 19:23; Ps. 25:14; Ps. 34:9; Ps. 86:11; 2 Cor. 7:1.

38

Keep your Faith and Trust in Jesus

Memorize

Mark 9:23 "Jesus said unto him, If you can believe, all things are possible to him that believes."

If you read the gospels —as I hope you are doing— you will notice that many times Jesus commands his disciples to have faith in Him. Jesus is the same yesterday, today, and forever (Heb. 13:8); therefore, what He commanded His disciples 2,000 years ago, He commands His disciples today. But what Jesus commands is for our good. If we are able to believe in Jesus' promises, we will have an abundant and happy life here, and eternal life. You and I are followers of Jesus, and He wants to do good for us, but to do good for us, it is necessary to always believe in Him.

❓ Introductory Questions

1. If you promise something to someone, what would you think of him or her if he/she doesn't believe you? Would you give him/her what you promised if he/she doesn't believe in you?
2. How do you think you can grow your faith in Jesus?
3. Why do you think people often don't believe in Jesus?

Bible Story (Mark 9:14-29)

Jesus was in a certain place and went to where his disciples were. There were many people around them and He asked them what was happening. Then one from the crowd spoke up and told Jesus that his son had an evil spirit, and that he had brought it to His disciples and they had not been able to drive it out. This evil spirit made the young man shake very violently and foam at the mouth. The father also explained to Jesus that his son had been in this condition since he was a child; and he begged Him to have mercy on him. Then Jesus said to him, "If you can believe, all things are possible to him who believes." And immediately the boy's father cried out, saying, "I believe; help my unbelief." After this, Jesus had mercy on the young man and on his father and cast out the demon.

Jesus wants us to have complete trust in Him, and to truly believe that He will solve any problem we have. Many different problems arise in life, but if we fully trust in the Lord, He will help us; the Word of God helps us to have faith in Jesus.

Illustration

Walter B. Knight wrote an account of the life of John Wesley in his book *Knight's Master Book of New Illustrations*. He said that one day he was walking by a man who was having troubles, and he expressed his doubt about God's goodness by saying, "I don't know what I'm going to do with all these worries and these problems."

At that very moment, they saw a cow that stuck its head over the top of a wall. Then John Wesley asked, "Do you know why that cow stuck its head over the top of the wall?" "Because it couldn't see through the wall," he added. "That's the same thing you should do, you should put your head over those problems and have faith in God that He will get you through them and you will be all right."

❓ Questions About the Class

1. What did Jesus command His disciples many times?
2. Why does Jesus want us to have faith in God?
3. What was the problem in the Bible Story?
4. What did Jesus say to the boy's father?
5. What does the Bible Story teach us?
6. What should we do when we have problems according to the illustration?
7. What will happen to your life if you keep your faith in Jesus and in His Word? How can you make your faith grow?

Phrases to Memorize

1. God commands us to believe in His promises and not be afraid of the difficulties of this life.
2. The Lord wants us to have an abundant life, and to do so we need to believe His Word.
3. The way we can grow our faith is by constantly reading the Bible.
4. When we have problems, it is not the best time to strengthen our faith, because this is a daily task. Every day we must strengthen our faith with the Word of God, in order to be strong for the days when we have problems.

Other Bible passages on the theme for reading and memorization

Mt. 21:22; Heb. 11:6; Rom. 10:17; Heb. 11:1; Mk. 11:22-24; 2 Cor. 5:7; Prov. 3:5-6; Lk. 1:37; 1 Cor. 2:5; Phil. 4:13; Heb. 11:1-39; Mt. 17:20; Jas. 1:5-8; Gal. 2:20; 1 Cor. 16:13; 1 Jn. 5:4; Mk. 10:52; Rom. 1:17.

39

Watch your Thoughts

Memorize

Proverbs 12:5 "The thoughts of the righteous are right: but the counsels of the wicked are deceit."

One of the most difficult things in life is to learn to discipline our thoughts. If you learn this from a young age, you will be a very successful person in life. The Bible commands us to think about eight things: what is true; what is honorable; what is just; what is pure; what is lovely; what is admirable; what is excellent; and in general, everything that makes the Name of God more exalted (Phil. 4:8). The Bible is the Word of God, and the thoughts of the Lord must be ours. If we are filled with the Holy Spirit, our mind will be filled with the thoughts of God.

Introductory Questions

1. Why do you think our thoughts are so important?
2. How can you know how and what a person thinks?
3. What is having *good thoughts*? What happens when a person has good thoughts?

Bible Story (Deuteronomy 31:1-33:29)

Good thoughts are the thoughts of Jesus. Jesus always thought in faith, that is, he had complete confidence in God. He also thought about always doing good to others and helping them; he thought about spiritual things, not earthly things; his mind is a mind focused on God and on all that He is. If you keep your mind on Christ Jesus, on spiritual things and not on earthly things, your thoughts will be like His. It is normal for us to think about the things of this life, but our delight should be to constantly think about the Lord.

One of the examples we have of a man who constantly kept his thoughts on God was Moses. There was a moment in Moses' life when he made a mistake, he sinned before God because of a fit of anger; and that sin did not allow him to enter the promised land. Imagine that you are struggling to achieve something, and you spend your whole life fighting for it, and in the end, because of a single mistake, everything goes to waste. How would you feel? Many people who have experienced something like this, their life becomes bitter and their thoughts become gloomy; but that was not what happened to Moses. Moses continued to obey the Lord, he brought Joshua, he made him his successor, he blessed him, and he also blessed the people of Israel; Moses' thought was only to please God and that was the center of his life.

Illustration

Mark Batterson wrote the following account in his book called *In a Pit with a Lion on a Snowy Day*: Drs. Avi Karni and Leslie Ungerleider of the National Institute of Mental Health did a fascinating study. They had a person do a simple task: type with a single finger every day for four weeks. Then, when they scanned that person's brain, they saw that the area of the brain that did that task had grown. New cells had literally been added.

This story teaches us that when we read the Bible we are adding cells with the thought of God to our brain; literally our brains are making new and amazing connections with the thought of Christ, that is the way to develop the mind of Christ in us.

❓ Questions About the Class

1. What are the eight things God commands us to think about? (Name at least three).
2. How can we know God's thoughts?
3. How does the Holy Spirit intervene in us to help us think good thoughts?
4. What did Jesus think?
5. What should you keep your mind on?
6. How does Moses' life give us a good example of God-centered thinking?
7. What does the illustration teach us?

Phrases to Memorize

1. God commands us to think of whatever is true, whatever is honorable, whatever is just, whatever is pure, whatever is lovely, whatever is admirable, whatever is excellent, and whatever brings high the name of God.
2. How we think, what is in our hearts, is what determines our words and actions, that is why it is so important.
3. Jesus always thought in faith, He had complete confidence in God, and His mind was on spiritual things, not on earthly things, like us.
4. The only way we can have a mind like Jesus is by constantly reading, memorizing, and meditating on the Holy Scriptures.

Other Bible passages on the theme for reading and memorization

Phil. 4:8; Prov. 17:22; Phil. 4:6; Jer. 29:11; Eph. 4:31-32; Mt. 21:22; Mt. 15:18-20; Rom. 12:2; Prov. 15:1; Jn. 14:27; Heb. 13:6; 2 Cor. 10:5; Prov. 4:23; Prov. 6:16-18; Prov. 12:2; Prov. 12:5; Prov. 21:4-5.

40

The Great Commission

Memorize

Matthew 28:19 "Go ye therefore, and teach all nations, baptizing them in the name of the Father, and the Son, and the Holy Ghost".

The will of the Lord Jesus is that all people believe in Him and enter heaven. However, in order for them to believe, God has commanded us to be the ones to preach to them. No person can be saved if we do not preach Jesus, and you and I have the great responsibility of preaching to them and teaching them the Word of God. Do you talk about Jesus to your schoolmates? Do they know that you are a Christian?

? Introductory Questions

1. When was the last time you talked about Jesus to someone?
2. What happens when you talk about Jesus?
3. What is necessary for someone to become a Christian?

Bible Story (John 3:1-15)

A man came to visit Jesus at night. His name was Nicodemus and he was a Pharisee. Why do you think Nicodemus went to Jesus at night? When he was in front of Jesus, he told him that he recognized that He had come from God. Immediately, Jesus told him that it was necessary for him to be *born again* in order to enter heaven. Do you know what being born again is? Jesus told him something that Nicodemus was unaware of. He thought —like many in this world— that he needed to do certain works to enter heaven, but Jesus' message was one of *repentance and faith*. Do you know what the word repentance means? Repentance is recognizing our sin before God, asking for forgiveness with all our heart, and turning away from evil. It also implies forgiving those who have offended us. After we do this, what follows is seeing with our spiritual eyes the love of God in Christ Jesus, when He died on the cross for our sins. This passage speaks of it: "And as Moses lifted up the serpent in the wilderness, even so must the Son of Man be lifted up: that whosoever believeth in him should not perish, but have everlasting life" (v. 14-15). So, the only thing that is needed to do after repentance is to believe that Jesus is your only and sufficient Savior and make Him the Lord of your life. Then you will be born again! Have you already been born again? If not, ask your teacher to guide you to Jesus to be born again and you will be a new creature in Jesus.

Illustration

George Sweeting published the story of John Currier in his book *The No Guilt Guide to Witnessing*. John Currier was convicted of murder in 1949 and sentenced to life in prison. However, he was later allowed to work for free on a farm near Nashville, Tennessee. But he was still not free.

Twenty years later, in 1968, the authorities determined that John did not need any further punishment, and they sent him a letter asking for his release. Life on the farm was very hard, and John had no hope of getting out, because he thought he had been sentenced to life in prison; therefore, the letter would be wonderful news for him. However, the letter never arrived, and John remained working in that farm for many more years. What do you think of those who should have given the letter to John? We have been commissioned by God to give this Good News: "Jesus has already died for your sins on the cross, you do not need to remain enslaved to sin." But if we do not give this Good News to those who have not been born again, the sinners will continue on their way to hell. Would you like to pray that God will help you fulfill the Great Commission?

Questions About the Class

1. What is the Great Commission that Jesus left us?
2. What is the will of the Lord according to what we have seen in the lesson?
3. What is necessary for a person to believe in Jesus?
4. What was the name of the man who came to visit Jesus at night? What did Jesus say to him?
5. What does it mean to be born again?
6. What is needed to be born again?
7. What does the illustration seen in class teach us?

Phrases to Memorize

1. The Great Commission that Jesus gave to all Christians is to preach Jesus and teach them the Word of God.
2. God's will is for everyone to be saved, but for that to happen it is necessary that we speak to them about the Lord.
3. Being *born again* means that a person becomes a disciple of Jesus, that is, he makes Jesus his Savior and the Lord of his life.
4. To be born again or to be saved, two things are needed: *repentance and faith in Jesus.*
5. Repentance means recognizing the sin we have committed, asking the Lord for forgiveness with all our heart and turning away from evil; it also implies forgiving those who have offended us.

Other Bible passages on the theme for reading and memorization

Mt. 28:18-20; Mk. 16:15; Jn. 20:21; Is. 6:8; Acts. 1:8; Lk. 24:46-47; Rom. 10:15; Jn. 4:35-38; Lk. 10:1-12; 2 Ti. 2:15; Rom. 1:16; Rev. 7:9; Acts. 22:21; Acts. 2:28; Lk. 12:9.

Other Resources: Visit Jesusfilm.org for resources and tips for preaching Jesus and fulfilling the Great Commission.

41

Main Types of Prayer

Memorize

Mark 11:24 "Therefore I tell you, whatever you ask for in prayer, believe that you have received it, and it will be yours."

Prayer is the only instrument we have from God to communicate with Him through Jesus. Every Christian prays, and praying is to him or her what breathing is to the human body. We need God at every moment, and from Him, we receive everything we are and everything we have. God gives us all things freely, and the only thing He requires of us is that we ask in faith. Sin is always an obstacle to our prayers, therefore, we have to live a life of holiness; but the life of prayer (together with the Word of God) helps us to live in that Holiness. There are three general types of prayer that you should practice constantly.

Introductory Questions

1. Why do you think it is important to pray in the morning before you start your day?
2. Can you give us a testimony of a prayer that God has answered?
3. Do you like to communicate with your earthly father/mother? How is this communication similar to prayer?

Explanation

We have much to learn regarding the subject of prayer. Jesus taught His disciples to pray in Matthew 6 and Luke 11, and the model prayer is written there. It includes worship and praise, and the following requests: that God's will be done, for physical provision, for fellowship with one another, for forgiveness of our sins, and for protection from all evil. We are to pray with faith, in Jesus' name, and always give thanks to God. We are to pray for ourselves and for others.

There are three types of prayer: 1) Group prayer (with our brothers in Christ); 2) private prayer (which we pray to God daily); and 3) unceasing prayer (which we pray constantly in our hearts and sometimes with words, but it is always short prayers throughout the day and at every moment).

Three stories as an example (Acts 4:23-31; Daniel 9:1-23; Nehemiah 2:1-5)

1. The prayer of the persecuted disciples in Acts 4:23-31 is an example of group prayer. They were being persecuted by the Jews and religious leaders, so they asked the Lord to help them. God answered their prayer by sending the Holy Spirit upon them.

SPIRITUAL RESILIENCE

2. We have many examples of private prayer. One of them was the case of Daniel 9, where the prophet Daniel prays interceding for his people, for Israel. The Lord's answer came after Daniel had been praying for 21 days.

3. We have an example of praying without ceasing in Nehemiah 2:1-5. Nehemiah had been praying about the terrible situation in Jerusalem and its walls. And when the king said to him, "What do you ask?" he prayed a little prayer to God. The Christian is always praying to God, whether in his heart, in a babbling voice, or even in words. These are short prayers and they are all the time (in addition to his private prayer alone with God and his group prayer).

Illustration

In 1842, Charles Dickens, already a famous writer, attended a Christian church in Boston, Massachusetts. There, he heard an impassioned prayer calling for the abolition of slavery. This experience had such a profound impact on Dickens that in that same year he began to write and advocate more intensely against slavery and social injustices.

Charles Dickens' experience in Boston strengthened his convictions and made him believe that deep, intense prayer before God changes things. Thus, 23 years later, in 1865, slavery was abolished in the United States. God answered prayer.

Questions About the Class

1. What can prayer be compared to when we speak of the life of the human body?
2. What does God ask us to have when we pray?
3. Why is it very important to live in holiness in order to receive answers to our prayers?
4. What are the three general types of prayer?
5. What are the themes included in the model prayer of Matthew 6 and Luke 11?
6. What is the prayer without ceasing (1 Thess. 5:11)? Give a biblical example for each type of prayer.

Phrases to Memorize

1. Prayer is to the Christian what breathing is to the physical body.
2. God gives us everything freely, and all he asks of us is that we have faith.
3. Sin is an obstacle to our prayers, but prayer also helps us to live without sin.
4. The three types of prayers that we should practice are these: group prayer; daily private prayer; and continuous prayer.
5. Jesus' prayer in Matthew 6 and Luke 11 serves as a model for our daily prayers.

Other Bible passages on the theme for reading and memorization

Jn. 15:7; Mt. 6:6-7; Rom. 8:26; 1 Ts. 5:17; Jas. 5:16; Jer. 33:3; Lk. 11:9; Mt. 26:41; Eph. 6:18; Col. 4:2; 1 Ti. 2:1-4; Mt. 6:9-13; Jer. 29:12; Ps. 34:17; 1 Ti. 2:5; 1 Pet. 3:7.

42

Use AI Responsibly

Memorize

Philippians 4:8 "And now, dear brothers and sisters, one final thing. Fix your thoughts on what is true, and honorable, and right, and pure, and lovely, and admirable. Think about things that are excellent and worthy of praise."

You are probably familiar with artificial intelligence (AI). This is a concept that has become popular all over the world due to its great advantages in performing many tasks that we used to do ourselves. But have you ever thought about what are the dangers that exist when using this technology? The verse from Colossians helps us to have a compass regarding how we should use AI. In this class, you will learn a lot about this.

❓ Introductory Questions

1. How do you think AI is changing the world?
2. How do you think we can use AI to honor God with it?
3. How can you be sure that by using AI you are not cooperating with evil?

Bible Story (Job 4:7; 8:5-7; 11:13-19)

Until a few years ago, people used Google to find answers to their questions. Now they go to ChatGPT and many other AI websites to ask questions and search for information. Nevertheless, you need to know that they will not always tell you the truth. Why? Because AI systems analyze massive amounts of data and use algorithms to make decisions, but the majority of these data is coming from non-Christian sources. The second warning is this: AI is quickly making many people believe that human beings can be easily replaced, and this makes human beings look inferior. Regarding this, the Bible says that human beings were created by God and were created to be connected with other human beings, not with computers and machines that imitate them. This makes human beings lose dignity (remember, "everything worthy"). But that is not all. With AI, much evil can be done, and many evils can be invented (Rom. 1:30). What you see appears to be real, but it is not, it is a lie, and the devil is the father of lies (Jn. 8:44).

Keep in mind that the world system will always be against God (James 4:4), so if, for example, you ask ChatGPT to give you an opinion on a moral issue, you will notice that it tends to be against Christian concepts; if you ask it to give you the name of a person who is charitable, it will give you the name of a Muslim rather than a Christian, etc. AI could also be used to create inappropriate content, to manipulate information, and even to control others and invade their privacy. Excessive use of AI can also lead to people losing their jobs and creating social injustice. On the other hand, AI can be used responsibly, and be useful for preaching the gospel and teaching the Word of God. It can also be used for graphic design, business, data analysis, etc., but it should always be used responsibly and honestly, taking into account the well-being of others.

In the Job passages you read, Job's friends thought they were doing something right by judging Job, but their concept was false. So, you too may think you are doing the right thing when you are not, so you should always meditate on whether what you are doing is really something that pleases God or not, and ask your parents (if they are Christians) and your teachers at church.

Exercise

In this exercise, you and your classmates discuss the answers to these questions.

1. How could you use AI to help others seek and honor God?
2. How would you use AI to do a task, for example, but at the same time, you are using your mind to do it, so that you have integrity and don't present something that isn't yours as yours?
3. How do you think AI will affect people's jobs? Which ones do you think will no longer exist?
4. Would you trust AI to make decisions? Yes/no, why?
5. Do you think AI affects our privacy and personal data?
6. How do you imagine AI will play a role in end-time prophecies?

❓ Questions About the Class

1. What are some of the disadvantages seen in class of the use of AI?
2. How can AI be used to advance the gospel?
3. Why does AI have a tendency to discredit the gospel of Christ?
4. Can AI be used to generate inappropriate content, for example, sexual impurity?

Phrases to Memorize

1. AI can make you think that machines are a better alternative than humans and personal contact.
2. AI can be used irresponsibly and be an instrument to sin and promote sin in the world.
3. AI should never be used to make moral and spiritual decisions.
4. AI is not made by Christians and is part of the world's polluted system.
5. AI offers many good things, but we must think how to use with honesty to bless others and ourselves, while we are pleasing our God with it

Other Bible passages on the theme for reading and memorization

1 Ts. 2:4; Rom. 12:1-2; Heb. 11:6; Rom. 8:8; Gal. 1:10; Mk. 13:5; Jn. 7:7; Jn. 9:5; Jn. 15:18-19; Prov. 14:12; Col. 2:8; Gn. 1:26; Jas. 3:15.

Part V. Leadership Foundations

43

Racial Discrimination

Memorize

Acts 17:26 "God began by making one man, and from him he made all the different people who live everywhere in the world. He decided exactly when and where they would live."

Racism has existed throughout the history of mankind and even in the history of all religions. Racism is discrimination against a person or group because of their race; when a certain race believes it is superior to another. However, this has been forbidden by God from the beginning. It is true that God chose Israel so that the world would know about Him, but He did not choose them because they were a superior race, but because they were an insignificant people and slaves (Deut. 7:7). And in many passages God orders Israel to treat foreigners as themselves (e.g. Lev. 19:33-34).

❓ Introductory Questions

1. Do you think that others who are different from you are the same as you?
2. Should people who are different hang out with everyone else? Yes/No, why?
3. Do you think that a certain race is smarter than another?

Bible Story (2 Samuel 19:30-40)

Because of the evil of human beings, they have created barriers to divide us. They distinguish and label races and say that certain races are stronger than others or more intelligent or more educated than others; however, this is not true. Someone may tell you that black people, for example, are a cursed race and that they are the descendants of Ham (the son of Noah), but that is not true. All human beings are equal.

During Jesus' time, the Jews believed that they were a superior race because God had chosen them to be his instrument, and for that reason they discriminated against those who were not Jews. This idea was so strong that even the apostles held it. When Peter was staying at the house of a man named Simon (the tanner), God showed him a vision and made him understand that those who were not Jews were equal to the Jews. He also told him to go to the house of a Roman and preach about Jesus to him and his family. Peter then obeyed the Lord, and they received the Holy Spirit in the same way as the Jews. From then on, Peter and all the others who had believed in Jesus understood that God does not discriminate against anyone and does not want us to discriminate against anyone either.

Illustration

Our Daily Bread devotional published something that Mahatma Gandhi, the man who helped India gain independence from England, wrote in his autobiography. He wrote that when he was a student, he read the Gospels and was seriously considering becoming a Christian. He felt that Jesus' teachings solved the division that exists in his country due to discrimination (because in India there is a terrible problem of discrimination due to the religion they profess).

So Gandhi went to a Christian church near where he lived on Sunday, and when he tried to enter, the usher refused to let him sit inside the church, but told him to go and worship with his own people. Gandhi was very offended and said, "If Christians also discriminate against others, why should I become a Christian?" From then on, Gandhi gave up the idea of becoming a Christian.

❓ Questions About the Class

1. What are the problems that discrimination creates?
2. Why do you think Jews were racist, even though God had told them not to be?
3. What was Peter's idea of non-Jews?
4. What did God make Peter understand?
5. Why did Mahatma Gandhi want to become a Christian?
6. What discouraged Mahatma Gandhi from becoming a Christian?
7. Can you mention other kinds of discrimination that exists today?

Phrases to Memorize

1. We must never consider our race (or skin color) to be "better" than another.
2. Discrimination between people divides us, and that is a sin before God.
3. The Bible is God's book, and God teaches us from the beginning to love one another and treat others as ourselves, without considering their country of origin or their language or their skin color.
4. In heaven there will be people of all nations, of all languages, of all races and of all skin colors.
5. God does not discriminate between people and commands us to be like that too. Christians must imitate Jesus in everything.

Other Bible passages on the theme for reading and memorization

Gal. 3:28; Acts. 17:26; Jn. 7:24; Rom. 2:11; Acts. 10:34-35; Jn. 13:34; Rom. 10:12; Ap. 7:9; Jas. 2:9; Acts. 10:34; Gn. 1:26-27; 1 S. 16:7; Col. 3:11.

44

The Great Value of Work

Memorize

Ecclesiastes 2:24 "The best thing people can do is eat, drink, and enjoy the work they must do. I also saw that this comes from God."

When God put man in the Garden of Eden, He didn't put him there to do nothing. He gave him work. Adam's work was physical and intellectual. Adam's physical work was to work the garden, and his intellectual work was to name the animals. Genesis 2:15 says, "The Lord God took the man and put him in the Garden of Eden to work it and take care of it," and Genesis 2:19 says, "Out of the ground the Lord God formed every beast of the field and every bird of the air. He brought them to Adam to see what he would call them. Whatever Adam called every living creature, that was its name." In order for Adam to name each animal appropriately, he would have to observe them and think. So, work is one of the blessings God gave to mankind. God wants us to work at something good and be useful.

❓ Introductory Questions

1. How do you feel after doing a job well done?
2. To be completely honest, do you like to work? Did you know that work is very good for you?
3. What are the chores that your parents make you to do?

Bible Story (Acts 18:1-3)

In the Bible we have many cases of people who were very hard-working. They understood that work is a blessing from God that we can enjoy every day; furthermore, work is a responsibility. We all must work in some way, from the smallest to the oldest. People who work are healthy and strong, and they gain more blessing from God.

The apostle Paul was an extremely hard-working man. In addition to preaching and teaching the Word of God, he also worked at his trade: he made tents. Do you know what that is? In the times of the apostle Paul, many people lived in tents and he knew how to make them. He worked with his hands. This is how he met Priscilla and Aquila, a Christian couple who joined him, since they were in the same trade. Although Paul did not always work at his trade and preaching at the same time, he wanted to show everyone that Christians should work hard and earn their own bread, and also share with those in need.

Illustration

In 2009, Jamaican athlete Usain Bolt became the fastest man in the world. He ran the 100-meter dash in 9.58 seconds and to this day (2024), Bolt is the fastest man. Although the race he ran lasted less than ten seconds, it was nothing more than the result of many hours of hard work: training, a special diet, and constant discipline in every aspect. If you want to be an important person someday, you must learn that constant hard work is the characteristic of all who achieve success in any area. So too, in the Christian life, we must work with dedication in everything to which God calls us. But remember, you must also rest one day a week.

❓ Questions About the Class

1. What was the work that God gave to Adam when he was in the Garden of Eden?
2. The work that God gave to Adam was both physical and _____
3. Why can we say that the apostle Paul was a hard worker?
4. What were the jobs that the apostle Paul did? Why did the apostle Paul work? What purpose does working serve?
5. How did Usain Bolt become the fastest man in the world?
6. How should one work to be successful in life?

Phrases to Memorize

1. Honest and useful work is a blessing given by God from the beginning.
2. God wants us to work so that we feel useful and satisfied with our lives.
3. When we work, we receive rewards, and if we learn to work one day we will have enough for ourselves and to help others.
4. One of the characteristics of a successful person (like the apostle Paul) is hard and constant work.

Other Bible passages on the theme for reading and memorization

1 Cor. 4:12; Jn. 17:4; 1 Ti. 5:8; 1 Ts. 4:11; Gn. 3:19; 2 Ts. 3:7-9; Phil. 2:5-8; Jn. 5:17; Eph. 6:5; Acts. 18.1-3; Gn. 2:15; 1 Ti. 5:17; Jn. 9:4.

45

Giving for God

Memorize

Acts 20:35 "In all things I have shown you that by working hard in this way we must help the weak and remember the words of the Lord Jesus, how he himself said, 'It is more blessed to give than to receive.'"

In the verse you memorized, the apostle Paul is speaking. He repeats some words that the Lord Jesus said that are not in the gospels, but that were important for the world to know, that is why they were written in the Book of Acts. In these, Jesus says something that we should all remember: that when we work and earn money, it is not just for us to enjoy it ourselves, but that part of it should be given to God. Christians basically give for two causes: to support the preaching of the gospel (mostly for the local church) and for those in need. When we do this, the money we give is given to God Himself.

❓ Introductory Questions

1. What would you do if you suddenly received a lot of money?
2. What is something you have always wanted to buy but you don't have the money or your parents didn't have the money to buy it for you?
3. Do you think you are rich or poor? Do you think there are others who are poorer than you? Have you ever helped them?

Bible Story (Mark 12:41-44)

Jesus went to the temple and observed those who gave offerings. The Lord was not impressed by what the rich gave, because although they gave large amounts, they really gave what they had left over. But besides them, he saw a poor widow who put some money into the offering box. Widows in Bible times were almost always very poor, because it was the men who worked and she, if she did not have children to support her, had to live on charity.

What this poor widow gave was so little that it amounts to only a few cents in today's money, and it was possible to buy just a little bread with this. Jesus said that this woman had given all she had to eat, that is, she gave with great sacrifice.

When we give to support those who preach the Word of God to us and to the poor, we are obeying what God has told us. In this case, the poor widow gave to support the preaching of the gospel; and she did it for God, not for others to see her. Jesus says that if we give to receive approval and praise from others, we will not receive a reward from Him.

Illustration

Daniel Lioy told a very interesting story regarding giving in his International Bible Lesson Commentary 2008-2009. He says that the Marquis de Lafayette, a Frenchman who helped George Washington's army, returned to France after helping George and went back to his work as a farmer. 1783 was a terrible year for almost all the farmers in his country, but Lafayette's fields did just the opposite: they produced abundantly. Then one of the workers said to Lafayette, "Well, this is the time to sell," but Lafayette replied, "No, my friend, this is the time to give."

This story teaches us that we should always consider others who have been less fortunate than us. God has placed us to help other people who are poorer; there will always be someone poorer than you, and God wants you to use the resources He has given you to help them. Never speak ill of those who have less than you.

❓ Questions About the Class

1. Is God watching what you give to Him? Yes/no, why do you think what we give is important to God?
2. Why did Jesus speak well of the poor widow who gave to support the preaching of the gospel?
3. Why was what the widow gave really too much for her?
4. What are the two things that God wants us to give to constantly?
5. How did Lafayette think after what happened to the farmers in his country in 1783 while he did very well that same year?
6. What does this story teach us?

Phrases to Memorize

1. God commands us in His Word to give money to support those who preach His Word and to help the poor with our goods and money.
2. You may belong to a poor family, but there will always be someone poorer than you. Consider this when you receive some money or if you receive many gifts.
3. God does not see the amount we give, but if we do it with all our heart and if it is with sacrifice, God does not want you to give Him what is left over.
4. Never speak badly of those who are poorer than you, because you do not know enough about their lives, God commands us to give to them, not to judge them.
5. When you give, you should do it for God and not so that people see that you give.

Other Bible passages on the theme for reading and memorization

2 Cor. 9:7; Lk. 6:38; Acts. 20:35; Prov. 19:17; Mt. 6:1-4; 1 Ti. 5:8; 1 Ti. 6:10; Dt. 25:4; 1 Cor. 9:9; 1 Ti. 5:18; 1 Cor. 9:13; Lk. 10:7; Prov. 19:17.

46

Saving Money

Memorize

Proverbs 21:20 "The wise store up choice food and olive oil, but fools gulp theirs down."

God has appointed each of us as stewards. You will surely receive some amount of money in your life, it may be a lot or a little compared to others, but no matter how much it is, God wants you to be a good steward. A good steward knows how to strike a balance between giving, spending, and saving. As a general principle, God wants you to have enough for your own needs, and to share with others as well. However, every good steward knows that it is necessary to be careful about what you spend and to save so that you do not have to borrow later.

Introductory Questions

1. Do you know what debt is? Why does God want you not to borrow?
2. How much should you save? Do you have any idea? Share your thoughts.
3. How do you feel when you have some money in your possession? Do you feel like you own it or do you feel like you are God's steward?

Bible Story (John 6:1-12)

In John's passage we can read the story of the feeding of the five thousand men (not counting women and children), so there were perhaps eight thousand or more people. That is a large number of people, don't you think? We see there a need that the Lord Jesus mentioned, what was that need? Yes! Correct! They needed to eat, because they were hungry. You must learn to identify what is really necessary. Jesus said that what is most necessary is: 1) Shelter (having a place to live, and clothes to wear); 2) Clean water to drink; and 3) Food [Matthew 6:31-33]. In addition, there are other needs that no one could live without, can you mention some others? Then, we see that Jesus had compassion on the people; you too must have compassion on the people who are in need and help them. Finally, when he had helped them (performing the miracle of multiplying the five loaves and two fish that a boy like you had donated), he ordered the disciples to gather what was left over, and that nothing was to be wasted. God does not want us to waste or squander what He gives us, and one of the important principles of stewardship is to save. When you save, you will then be able to buy cash and will not need to borrow.

Illustration

There was a little ant and a grasshopper who were neighbors. It was summer and the little ant worked and worked every day, while the grasshopper spent his time enjoying life, playing and eating, singing and wasting time. One day, the grasshopper wanted to make fun of the grasshopper and said: "What are you doing so much every day? Why do you work and work? Look at me, I enjoy life, I waste time on what I want. You are a fool!" said the grasshopper. "I am working now because winter is coming," said the little ant, "and in the winter I and my family will have enough food, and we will be safe.

Time passed, and winter came. Then the little ant went into her house and shut the door. Then the grasshopper, having saved nothing, came knocking at the little ant's door and asked for something to eat. "Give me something to eat," said the grasshopper, "even if it is borrowed, I will pay you back when I can work. If you were the little ant, what would you do?"

Jesus said, "I must work the works of him that sent me, while it is day: the night comes, when no man can work" (John 9:4). What this story teaches us is that just as the little ant worked and saved so that she would be prepared for hard times and so that she would not have to borrow, so should you. The grasshopper had to come knocking on the little ant's door to ask for help.

Questions About the Class

1. What three characteristics does a good steward have? What does a good steward save for?
2. What needs does Jesus identify in Matthew 6:31-33?
3. What did Jesus do when he saw the people's need?
4. What did Jesus order after the people had eaten?
5. What was the little ant doing in the illustration? What was the grasshopper doing?
6. What happened when winter came?

Phrases to Memorize

1. God owns all that you have and will ever have, and you are just a steward.
2. A good steward keeps a balance between giving, spending, and saving.
3. The reason a good steward saves is so that he will not have to borrow in the future and will always have enough.
4. God wants you to have enough in all things and abound to give to others from what He has given you.
5. When you have a family, you must distinguish what is a need from what is not a need. You must provide for the needs of your family.

Other Bible passages on the theme for reading and memorization

Prov. 21:20; Prov. 13:11; Prov. 10:4-5; Prov. 13:22; Prov. 13:5; 1 Ti. 5:8; Prov. 6:6-8; Lk. 14:28; 1 Ti. 6:10; Rom. 13:8; Mt. 25:14-30; 2 Cor. 9:6; Acts. 20:35.

47

Spending Money

Memorize

Matthew 6:19 "Do not lay up for yourselves treasures on earth, where moth and rust destroy and where thieves break in and steal."

The most important and valuable things in life cannot be bought with money. God's salvation in Christ Jesus is free, the fruit of the Spirit, the baptism in the Spirit and all the gifts of the Spirit of God cannot be bought. Then come the blessings of health and family, all of which cannot be bought with money. We must always see money as a simple instrument to honor God; to maintain human life (ours and our family's), and as an instrument to help those in need and to support our ministry. Having money or buying things does not satisfy, only God brings true satisfaction. Therefore, we should never work for money or for material things, but always do everything as if it were for the Lord (read John 6:27, Col. 3:23). God wants us to depend on Him and not on our riches; therefore, although we should save with purpose and to avoid debt, we should not save with the purpose of depending on what we have saved, because that will not please God.

Introductory Questions

1. How do you feel if someone steals something from you?
2. Do you feel like you have enough clothes, toys, gadgets, etc.?
3. If someone asks you to account for what you have spent, do you get angry? Yes/No, why?
4. Do you like to compare what you have with what someone else has?

Bible Story (Exodus 16:1-36)

How you use money and how you think about it determines whether you are a greedy person or not. If you get angry when someone takes a little of yours; when you don't want to share with others; when you feel like you don't have enough; when you get angry when your mom or dad asks you to account for what you have spent; or if you compare what you have with what others have, all of these things are signs that you are not spending money well and that you love money more than God. God wants you to spend, but He wants to be the One to tell you what to spend it on, because He is the Lord of your life. The principle you must learn is that God wants you to depend on Him and not on material things (even if He gave them to you).

The people of Israel were hungry in the wilderness, but instead of thanking God for what they had received from Him, they complained. Nevertheless, God was patient with them and sent them food from heaven. This food was called *manna*. But He gave them instructions. He told them to take manna for only one day, and not to hoard it. The only exception was the day before the Lord's Day, the Sabbath. On that day they were to gather double.

This teaches us that we must depend on the Lord and use what He gives us as He wants and not as we want, because everything is from Him. Thus, it happened that the Israelites who took more than they should of manna, the excess became worms; and those who did not save when they should have saved, then went out to look for what to eat, and there was nothing.

Illustration

The New York Times published an article on April 10, 2016, about the Wendels family. The Wendels were perhaps the most powerful families in New York City at the beginning of the 20th century, their 150 properties may be worth more than 1 billion dollars today. John Wendels, the oldest brother of the family, was able to influence his six sisters so that they did not marry. They lived together in one of their properties, without electricity. They wore the same clothes every day (clothes that were out of fashion 50 years ago). Likewise, they, although they were the richest in New York, lived as if they were miserable. When the last of the sisters died in 1931, she had worn the same dress for 25 years, a dress that she had made herself. The Wendels are a sad example of those who do not spend money as they should spend it and live without trusting in Jesus; rather, they trust in their riches.

Questions About the Class

1. What are the most valuable things in life?
2. How should we view money?
3. Who is the only One who gives true satisfaction to a human being?
4. What are some signs that someone is greedy or loves money?
5. What does the Bible Story from Exodus 16 teach us?
6. What does the illustration for this lesson teach us?

Phrases to Memorize

1. The most valuable things in life cannot be bought with money, and only God can give them.
2. God wants us to depend on Him every day and not on what we have accumulated.
3. We must spend money on what we need and enjoy it, but always remember to share with those in need and support God's work; these last two things are more important than spending on ourselves.
4. We must never work only for money, but to please God.

Other Bible passages on the theme for reading and memorization

Prov. 22:7; 1 Ti. 6:10; Heb. 13:5; Prov. 13:22; Dt. 8:18; Prov. 13:11; Lk. 12:15; 1 Ti. 6:17; Prov. 3:9; Mt. 6:33; Mt. 6:19-21; Ecc. 5:10.

48

Seek to Serve, Not to Be Served

Memorize

Galatians 5:13 "...but by love serve one another."

Christ said that He came, not to be served but to serve. Most people think that being served is better than serving, and they are not happy if they have the need to serve others. When you are a Christian these concepts must be eliminated from your thinking, because like Christ, we are all on this earth to serve one another, and we serve with joy.

? Introductory Questions

1. What do you like more, being served or serving others?
2. How do you feel when you serve others?
3. What do you think of the Lord Jesus, who being King, came to serve us? How is this King different from the Kings of the world?

Bible Story (Genesis 24:7-27)

God made us born on this earth with a purpose of service. God wants us to serve others; and if we serve, then we will be happy to feel useful. We should not seek to be served but to serve, because when we serve, then we will be obeying the Lord, and He will bless us with joy and peace. In the world, it is taught that you should seek that others serve you, and that you should be the king or queen, but that is an idea of the devil, who wants human beings to treat one another badly. The world also has the idea that you should serve only for money; but God says that we should serve out of love, without looking for anything in return. To all who serve out of love, God will give even more than what they could have earned by serving for money. People who serve out of love for others are the best people.

This was the sign that Abraham's servant was looking for when he went to find a wife for Abraham's son Isaac. When Rebekah was willing to serve Abraham's servant and did even more than he asked of her, he understood that this was the woman God wanted for Isaac. Furthermore, she was a woman who had never slept with any man and never slept with anyone after she got married, except with her husband (Isaac). That was the best woman, a woman who had good conduct and served out of love. You too should have the goal, when later you look for a husband or wife, to look for a person like that.

Illustration

Dr. R. B Ouellette, pastor of the First Baptist Church of Bridgeport, MI, told the story of Billy Bray. Billy Bray was a miner who accepted Jesus Christ as his Savior and Lord when he was 29 years old. Before he was saved, he had lived a life of alcoholism and immorality. But when he was saved, he was a witness for Christ and told many about the Lord.

On one occasion, while he was growing some potatoes in his garden, he heard the devil say to him, "Billy, God doesn't love you. If He did, He wouldn't give you such small potatoes." But Billy was full of God and answered the devil, "You lying devil, I served you for many years, and you didn't give me a single potato. I served you with all my strength, and you gave me absolutely nothing for all my efforts." With this, Billy remembered that the burden of serving the Lord (serving others) is much lighter than the burden of serving the devil (the pleasures of the world). It is true what Jesus said: "For my yoke is easy, and my burden is light" (Mt. 11:30).

❓ Questions About the Class

1. What are we on this earth for according to the introduction of this lesson?
2. What was Jesus' example regarding service?
3. What happens to us when we serve others?
4. What is taught in the world regarding service and why is this concept contrary to the Word of God?
5. What is the reason we should serve? What is the attitude we should have when serving?
6. What was the sign that Abraham's servant was looking for when looking for a wife for Isaac?
7. What did Billy Bray answer the devil (according to the illustration)?

Phrases to Memorize

1. Christ came to serve and not to be served, so we did.
2. Serving others is something that brings joy and satisfaction in life, because we fulfill our purpose here.
3. We should not serve just for money, or for some personal interest, but for love.
4. When we serve, we should do it with joy.
5. People who serve and do more than what is asked of them are always the best, you should be like that and associate with those who are like that.
6. Your goal should be to one day marry a person who likes to serve, and does it for love and with joy.

Other Bible passages on the theme for reading and memorization

1 Pet. 4:10; Acts. 20:35; Gal. 5:13-14; Mt. 20:28; Lk. 6:38; Jn. 13:12-14; Mk. 9:35; Mt. 23:11; Mk. 10:44-45; Mt. 25:35-40; Mk. 10:45; Heb. 6:10; Eph. 2:10; Col. 3:23-24.

49

Keep your Promises

Memorize

Psalms 15:1,4 "Lord, who may dwell in your sacred tent? Who may live on your holy mountain? ... who keeps an oath even when it hurts, and does not change their mind;"

These two verses you have memorized speak of a person who is close to God. Being close to God is the most privileged and blessed place you can have in this life and in eternity. David, God's prophet, says that a person who is close to God will always keep his promises.

An oath is a solemn promise in the name of something considered valuable (e.g. heaven, or my mother, etc.). In the Old Testament, swearing was allowed because Christ had not yet come to the world; but when He came, He forbade it (see Mt. 5:33-37), so we should never swear, and the promises we make should be firm. This passage from Psalms says that even if you see that what you promised did not suit you, you will not stop fulfilling what you promised. That is why you should be very careful when promising things to God and others. However, making promises is also very necessary in life; every good Christian makes promises when necessary.

❓ Introductory Questions

1. When is it necessary to make a promise? Why do you think it is so important to keep your promises?
2. What do you think about a person who makes a promise and doesn't keep it?
3. What if you made a promise to do wrong? Should you keep it?

Bible Story (Joshua 9:1-27)

If ever (I hope this never happens) you make a promise to do harm to someone, you must immediately repent before God and ask forgiveness from the person to whom you promised such a thing. The promises that you must keep are the promises of good. A Christian always makes promises of good for everyone, but he also keeps them. That is something very important in a person, because it speaks of a trustworthy and truthful person.

God gave the people of Israel the promised land, remember? But they had to fight and conquer it. They were gaining ground and their battles were God's battles, the only holy battles. But the citizens of Gibeon were very clever. They knew that God had commanded them to kill everyone, so they went to Joshua and pretended that they were from a very far away country and made him and the people promise not to harm them. Then the Israelites realized that they were their neighbors, a city where they had to kill the inhabitants. However, because of the promise they had made, they could not kill them. All this happened because neither Joshua nor the Israelites consulted God about this matter. You should always ask God before making any promise.

Illustration

Two brothers had some eggs that they were going to boil and eat. The older brother made a proposition and a promise to his younger brother. He said, "Little brother, if you let me smash these three eggs on your head I will give you a dollar." "It's a promise," said the younger brother. "Yes, I promise you that," said the older brother.

The younger brother agreed. Then the other took an egg and smashed it on his brother's head, and then the second. And there he stopped. The younger brother's head and clothes were all splattered with the first two eggs, and the younger brother was waiting for the third. Finally, the younger brother, gesturing, asked, "And the third? When are you going to smash the third one for me?" "Never," said the other brother, "the third one would cost me a dollar."

Questions About the Class

1. What is the best place you can have in this life and in eternity?
2. What does David say is necessary to be in that place?
3. What is the difference between a promise and an oath?
4. Are Christians allowed to swear? Yes/No, why?
5. What kind of promises should you never make? What should you do if you ever make them?
6. Is it important to make promises? Why is it so important to keep them?
7. Why did Joshua and the Israelites make a mistake in making a promise to the people of Gibeon?

Phrases to Memorize

1. A person who is close to God will always keep his promises.
2. Christians have been forbidden to swear because Christians always tell the truth.
3. You must be very careful when making a promise and ask God before making it.
4. An important person has to make many promises, but he always keeps them.
5. You should only make good promises; and not take advantage of those who are smaller than you.

Other Bible passages on the theme for reading and memorization

Nm. 30:2; Ps. 89:34; Eccl. 5:4-5; Mt. 5:37; Nm. 23:19; Jas. 5:12; 2 Cor. 1:19-20; Prov. 20:25; Jas. 1:5; Ps. 15:4; Prov. 11:3; Dt. 23:21-23; Prov. 25:14.

50
Obey your Authorities

Memorize

Romans 13:1 "Let everyone be subject to the governing authorities, for there is no authority except that which God has established. The authorities that exist have been established by God."

It is true that there are evil and corrupt authorities; authorities that are unjust and abuse their authority; however, as Christians, God commands us to submit to the authorities in everything that is not sin. You and I have authorities to whom we must be subject: our parents, school teachers, police officers, pastors, Sunday school teachers, and others. That is, in four main areas: in the family; at school or work; in government; and in the church. And God is above all.

Introductory Questions

1. Why do you think it is difficult for many people to obey authorities?
2. What happens if you disobey authorities, for example, if you commit a crime?
3. What would the world be like if there were no authorities? Give your opinion?

Bible Story (Matthew 8:5-13)

The authorities have been put there by God to protect us from evil; it is like an umbrella of protection that we have if we submit to it. But if we rebel, then the protection will be taken away; and not only that of that authority, but the protection of the one who is *above* it, that is, God. We must submit, but not if that authority orders us to do something contrary to God's law.

Jesus went to a town called Capernaum, where a man came to him whose servant was sick. The man knelt at his feet and begged him to be healed. The man was someone important; he was the leader of a group of 100 Roman soldiers (such people were called centurions). Then Jesus said to him, "I will go and heal him." But the centurion said to him, "Sir, I am not worthy that you should come under my roof. Just say the word, and my servant will be healed. For I, too, am a man under authority, with soldiers under me. I say to one, 'Go,' and he goes; and to another, 'Come,' and he comes." When he said this, Jesus commended his faith and said to him, "Go, and as you have believed, so be it done for you."

Here the centurion was sure of Jesus' spiritual authority and submitted himself totally to it, and then he received the miracle from Jesus. Every time we submit to divine authority, and to the authority delegated by God, we are acting with faith in God. The reason why the Christian can cast out demons in the name of Jesus is because Christ has given that authority to believers (Mark 16:17).

Illustration

Max Lucado wrote in his book *In the Eye of the Storm* the following: A naval ship of the United States fleet was sailing in a very stormy weather with very poor visibility. It was night, and the lookout reported: "Light heading to starboard (the sea to the right of the ship). The captain asked: "Is it moving or is it stationary." "It is not moving, captain." Then the captain ordered the sailor: "Order that ship to move, because we are heading for it." The sailor followed the captain's orders, and received this answer: "You better move." Upon receiving this answer, the captain became furious, took the microphone, and said: "Listen, I am the captain of a ship of the United States Navy, I order you to move, otherwise, the consequences will be disastrous for you." Then came the answer: "I am the lookout of the lighthouse that you are about to crash into." Then the captain said: "We are changing course, quickly." The lighthouse represents Christ, He is the one who gives the orders, He is the highest authority.

This story also illustrates that we all have an authority to which we must submit. In the home, the leader is the father, but the authority of the children is both the mother and the father (and these two need to be in agreement). The pastor is subject to the city judge. But, in the church, that judge is under the authority of his pastor. If the judge exceeds the speed limit when driving, he has to submit to the authority of the policeman by telling him to stop. Everyone must exercise their authority in love and kindness; not as lords or masters of the will of others, just as Jesus did.

❓ Questions About the Class

1. What are the authorities given by God?
2. How is authority related to faith?
3. Why can Christians cast out demons in the name of Jesus?
4. Why was the captain of the illustration the one who had to obey?
5. What does this story also teach us?
6. What happens if we rebel against the authority given by God?

Phrases to Memorize

1. Authorities have been established by God for our good.
2. Authorities are in four main areas: the family; school or work; government; and the church.
3. We will have many benefits if we submit to the authority given by God, mostly we will have the protection given by that authority and by God himself.
4. It is very dangerous to rebel against the authority established by God, because we could be entering into the enemy's territory.
5. We cannot submit to authority when it orders us to do something contrary to the law of God.

Other Bible passages on the theme for reading and memorization

Heb. 13:17; Rom. 13:1-2; Tit. 3:1; 1 Pet. 2:13-15; Eph. 6:1-4; Mt. 28:18; 1 Ti. 6:1-21; Mt. 22:21; Eph. 5:21; Jn. 19:11; Tit. 3:1-2; Jas. 4:7; Mt. 8:7-9; Acts. 4:19.

51

Discipline

Memorize

Proverbs 13:24 "Whoever spares the rod hates their children, but the one who loves their children is careful to discipline them."

Every person, because of original sin (of Adam and Eve) has the tendency to evil; and this evil includes not submitting to any authority. When a person does evil, his evil does not stop, but continues to grow until he does very bad things. The reason for discipline is to prevent your behavior from becoming more and more evil, and one day you will have to go to jail because you have committed a serious crime. Parents are the authority placed by God to help you shape your character and prevent evil from growing in you.

? Introductory Questions

1. Have your parents ever punished you? How do you feel after receiving the punishment?
2. What would happen if parents did not punish their children?
3. Do you think you needed to be disciplined when you were disciplined?

Bible Story (2 Samuel 15:7-18:33)

David was a very prominent servant of God. He wrote about half of all the Psalms and prophesied about the Savior, Jesus Christ. However, even though David was a man greatly loved by the Lord, he did not obey the Lord's command to discipline his children. So, since God is no respecter of persons, the consequences of this came to him

The most serious case against David's kingdom did not come from of one of his generals, nor one of the influential men of the kingdom, but do you know from whom? Yes, you answered correctly! It came from one of his sons: Absalom. Absalom wanted to take the kingdom from his own father and reign in his place; he was willing to kill the one who fathered him to be the king of Israel. Fortunately, God had mercy on David, and Absalom could not do what he planned, and he was the one who ended up dead. Nevertheless, with all this, David went through the greatest anguish of his life and lost a son. Why did all this happen? Because David was weak in disciplining his children, and this caused Absalom's rebellion to end in a great tragedy. This is what happens with parents who do not discipline their children. If you are disciplined by your father and mother, you have a very great reason to be grateful to the Lord, because this discipline will keep you from death.

Illustration

Benjamin Spock (1903-1998) was a highly influential American psychologist and pediatrician. He published a book called *Baby and Child Care* in 1946, and within the first six months, it had already sold half a million copies. One of his colleagues, Dr. Maier, even said that by the day of his death, he had sold more than 50 million copies of the book.

In his book, Mr. Spock advises parents not to discipline their children so as not to "harm them." However, later realizing the dire consequences of his advice, he wrote: "We have raised a generation of ill-mannered children. Parents are not firm enough with their children for fear of losing their love or of being resentful of them. This has been something that we professionals have demanded of parents, and although we did so with the best of intentions, we did not realize —until now— that our know-it-all attitude was damaging parents' self-confidence." Mr. Spock's statement should be a warning to the world today, a world where parents do not discipline their children, even though this idea contradicts the Word of God. God is never wrong, but men (even with all their knowledge) are.

❓ Questions About the Class

1. If a child does wrong and is not disciplined, can he correct himself?
2. Why is discipline necessary for children?
3. Who is God's authority to help you grow up healthy and without doing wrong?
4. What was the mistake that David made with his children?
5. What was the end of Absalom? Why did that happen to him?
6. What did the man who changed the education of children in the United States say (contradicting the Word of God)?

Phrases to Memorize

1. The Bible says that parents who do not discipline their children show that they do not love them.
2. A child who is not disciplined from a young age will be more likely to do very bad things in the future.
3. Parents are the authority placed by God to discipline children so that they grow well.
4. A father (like David) can be a servant of God and a strong person in other areas, but weak when it comes to disciplining his children.
5. The most outstanding psychologists have had to admit that what the Bible says is correct.

Other Bible passages on the theme for reading and memorization

Prov. 13:24; Heb. 12:5-11; Prov. 22:6; Prov. 23:13-15; Eph. 6:4; Prov. 22:15; Prov. 29:17; Prov. 19:18; Prov. 29:15; Prov. 12:1; Col. 3:21; Prov. 13:1; Prov. 15:32; Prov. 6:23; Prov. 10:17.

52

Your Talents

Memorize

Colossians 3:23 "Whatever you do, work at it with all your heart, as working for the Lord, not for human masters."

God created all things, and all living things. God's design allows for each thing to have its place and each living thing to have its function. Everything God has created is wonderfully perfect and when all creation fulfills its function, then there is complete harmony. The human body, family, society, and God's church function in the same way: each part has his/her talent and his/her function, and it is the responsibility of each to do his/her part. Even the functions that we may consider the simplest are really important, and God uses each one for His glory. Therefore, God gave each one a talent (or several talents) and we must all use what we have received from God for His glory.

❓ Introductory Questions

1. Do you know what talent(s) you have received from God? Have you asked your parents and friends what you are good at?
2. How are you using the talent you have received for the glory of God?
3. Would you like to have the talent that another person has? Who? Why or for what purpose would you like to have that talent?

Bible Story (Matthew 25:14-30)

Jesus told the story of a rich man who gave his possessions to his servants to manage. To one he gave five talents, to another two, and to another one; each according to his ability. God has not given you more than you can manage or anything that is beyond your ability. You must also learn that you must focus on what you are good at. Sometimes some waste their time and life trying to do things that they are not good at and do not have enough talent for; they should stop wasting time and dedicate themselves to developing the talents that they have truly received from God.

Now, Jesus said that after some time, the rich man returned and demanded an account from his servants. What happened was that those to whom he had given five and two had earned twice as much, and their master said to them, "Well done, good and faithful servant! You have been faithful over a few things, I will put you in charge of many things; enter into the joy of your master." But the one to whom he gave one talent made excuses and gave him back the talent his master had given him. For this reason, the latter was expelled and thrown into the outer darkness. This will also happen to those who do not put to work the talent that God has given them.

Illustration

In his book *Discover Your True Potential*, R. Ian Symour wrote the story of a young Greek man who could neither read nor write, who, being very poor, applied for a job as a janitor in a company in Athens. At first, he was the favorite of the recruiter because he was so friendly, helpful and self-confident, but when he interviewed him and realized that he could neither read nor write, he was immediately rejected. The young man, sad and disappointed, sailed to England. In England, having great talent for business, he became a very rich man. So, after some time, a famous newspaper wanted to interview him to talk about his achievements, and asked him to write his autobiography; but he told them: "I don't think that will be possible, because I can neither read nor write." The reporter, astonished, replied: "It's incredible! How much more you would have achieved if you knew how!" But the now rich man replied: "If I could read and write, now I would be a janitor in a company in Athens."

This story is not meant to teach you not to study, on the contrary, you should study as much as you can. However, the important thing about this story, and what you should always remember, is that it is not society that will dictate what you should do in life, but God. He was the one who created you and gave you a talent, and it is He who has determined what you should dedicate your life to. Therefore, you should always concentrate all your energies on developing the talent that you have received from God.

Questions About the Class

1. Who is it that has given you the talents you have? What purpose did he give them to you for?
2. Do you think your talent is necessary? Yes/no, why?
3. What report did those who received five and two talents give? What benefit did they get from developing their talents for their master?
4. What were the consequences suffered by the lazy or useless servant?
5. Why is it better to concentrate on what you are good at?
6. What is the most important lesson from the illustration?

Phrases to Memorize

1. God's design is perfect, so you should be very happy and grateful for the talent you have received from God and not think that someone else has a "better" talent than you.
2. You should set yourself the goal of discovering what you are good at and focus on this.
3. God will hold us accountable for the talents we have received from Him, we must use them to serve others.
4. You must work hard to develop the talent you have received from God.

Other Bible passages on the theme for reading and memorization

1 Cor. 4:2; 1 Pet. 4:10-11; 1 Ti. 5:8; Ps. 24:1; 1 Cor. 12:4-6; Mt. 25:14-30; 1 Cor. 10:31; Jas. 1:17; Rom. 12:6-8; 1 Ti. 4:14; Exo. 35:10; 2 Ti. 1:6; Mt. 5:14-16.

53

Learn to Plan

Memorize

Proverbs 3:5-6 "Trust in the Lord with all your heart and lean not on your own understanding; in all your ways submit to him, and he will make your paths straight."

There is a big difference in the way God's children plan. God's children pray for God's will to be done, and it is the Lord, through His Holy Spirit, who is directing them. You must learn to always make plans based on God's will; and you will find this will in the Bible (first of all); in the counsel of your parents; in that of your pastor, and in your personal prayer (when God speaks to your heart). However, after you plan something, at any time the Lord can change the plans according to His will. Nevertheless, you must always make plans.

? Introductory Questions

1. What are the most important things you should plan in your life?
2. Why do you think it is very important to be humble when you are going to plan something? (Read James 4:13-17).
3. What is the correct attitude you should take when plans do not turn out as you planned?

Bible Story (Acts 16:1-10)

Christ said that if someone wants to build a tower, he needs to calculate the cost, otherwise, if he does not plan, he may not be able to finish it, and everyone who sees it unfinished will make fun of him. He said this after talking about how much it costs to follow Him. This means that if you want to be a follower of Jesus, you have to follow the plans He has for you, because you will not be able to make your plans without Him, and He will be the one who tells you where to go.

A clear example of this is found in Acts 16:1-10. Paul, Silas, and Luke were excited about preaching the gospel and seeing all that the Holy Spirit was doing, so they made plans to go to Asia to preach. However, the Holy Spirit spoke to them and forbade them to preach there. They made plans again; this time they planned to go to Bithynia, and the Holy Spirit once again told them that it was not His will for them to go at that time. So, they decided to be still and pray until the Lord showed them where He wanted them to go. They were in the midst of this when Paul had a vision of a man from Macedonia inviting him to go there. That was God's plan! Then, they happily went where God was calling them. In this story we can learn that while it is important for us to make plans, we must be sure that these plans are what the Holy Spirit has for us.

Illustration

During the American Civil War, a group of pastors invited Abraham Lincoln to breakfast. Abraham Lincoln was a man of great faith, although sometimes a little different from others. Before they began to eat, a pastor said to him, "Mr. President, let us pray that God will be on our side," but Mr. Lincoln replied, "No, sir, let us pray that we will be on God's side." This illustration teaches us that if we make plans and want God to back them up, they will have little chance of success, but if we let God show us His plans and direct our lives, He will be with us and everything will turn out well. You need to make plans, but you have to be sure that those plans are the ones God has for you. Sometimes those plans may seem illogical to the world, but God always knows what He is doing. However, as a general rule, you must use intelligence and wisdom to make plans.

Questions About the Class

1. Is the way God's children plan the same as the way the world plans? Yes/No, why?
2. What is the prayer you should pray before planning anything?
3. Where can you find God's will for your plans?
4. What did Christ say about the one who wanted to build a tower? What did He mean by that?
5. Why, if Paul and his companions planned to go to Asia and Bithynia, did they not go at that time?
6. What did Paul and his companions do to learn God's plan?
7. Tell us the illustration's story, what is the lesson we have there?

Phrases to Memorize

1. Those who follow Jesus always pray for God's will to be done in their lives and plan by putting God first. They also say, "if the Lord wills..."
2. God's will is in the Bible first, then in the advice of your parents; then in the advice of your leaders in the church (mature and wise Christians).
3. A follower of Jesus is led by the Holy Spirit and the Holy Spirit is like the wind (read John 3:8; also 1 Kings 18:8-12), so you need to pray always for the guidance of the Holy Spirit.
4. God's plans for you are greater than you can imagine, and these are the best for you, regardless of what others think.
5. Even the most devoted men to God have planned wrong. You too, at times may plan wrong, but do not be afraid to make changes if God wants it that way.

Other Bible passages on the theme for reading and memorization

Prov. 21:5; Prov. 16:9; Lk. 14:28-33; Prov. 3:5-6; Jer. 29:11; Prov. 24:27; Prov. 15.22; Prov. 6:6-8; Prov. 19:21; Jas. 4.13-15; Prov. 11:14; Rom. 8:28; Prov. 14:8.

54

Learn to say NO!

Memorize

Proverbs 1:10 "My son, if sinners entice you, do not consent."

The word no is a very small word, but one of the most powerful words that exist. God has given you the power to say *no*, and your free decision is very powerful. Human beings will always want to scare you and force you to do what they want, but you always have the power to say no and walk away from them. One of the most important things in life is knowing how to say no when it is necessary, this is what this lesson is about.

❓ Introductory Questions

1. Have you ever been forced to say yes when you really didn't want to?
2. Have you ever had someone ask you for a favor, and you promised to serve them when you really couldn't?
3. When someone asks you for something or offers you something, do you keep in mind your priorities? Do you ask for time to think about it?

Bible Story (Nehemiah 6:1-11)

In the world, you will encounter people who pressure others to do what they want. However, remember that you, as a Christian, have the Holy Spirit, and He makes you a person of strong character (read 2 Tim. 1:7). Some people start doing you favors so that you feel obligated or indebted to them. However, if what they offer or propose to you is against the Word of God, or goes beyond your limits, you must say no, even if they have done you many favors before. Remember that people who truly love you do not ask you for anything in return.

Some people insist even though you have told them no. But remember that Jesus said that your yes should be yes and your no should be no (Mt. 5:37); therefore, you must be firm. If you need time to decide (e.g., you need to ask your parents' permission or if you are going to think about whether you can really do it) you must ask for that time. But when you say no, you must be firm in what you have said, remembering that you are not obligated to give reasons for your decision. You will find that if you learn to say no, people will respect you, and you will be learning to be a leader. You need to be a leader in order to lead others to Christ.

Nehemiah is a good example of a resolute Christian. God gave him the task of rebuilding the walls of Jerusalem, but the enemies of God's people did everything they could to make him fail. His enemies tried to frighten him, but Nehemiah was a firm man. On one occasion, they threatened him, saying that they were coming to kill him, and that he needed to flee, that he needed to lock himself in the temple to save his life. But Nehemiah replied, "Should a man like me flee? Would someone like me go into the temple to save his life? I will not go in!" And Nehemiah was firm, and God was with him.

Illustration

At the time of World War II, the pastors and Christians in general in Germany did not have the courage to oppose Adolf Hitler, even though they knew all the bad things he did. However, there was a man named Dietrich Bonhoeffer; this man did not agree with Hitler and when he was invited to speak on the radio, he spoke against him and opposed him. The result of this was that he was taken to prison, and he, even though he was an extremely intelligent and prominent man in Germany, was hanged. Dietrich died because he said no! to what this evil and bloodthirsty man Hitler was doing. In life, you must say <u>no</u> to everything bad, to everything that is against the Word of God. You must say no to sin, and to people who want you to get involved with them and then do what you should not. You must also learn to say <u>no</u> when what someone asks of you is beyond what you can do or is something that is not convenient for you (for example, something that will make you waste time). Don't be afraid to say no. Later, you should also say no to job offers that don't match your gifts and talents.

Questions About the Class

1. What is a very powerful two-letter word that you can use as a great weapon in life? Why will it make you a strong-willed person if you use it properly?
2. What is a strategy that some people have to get you to say yes?
3. When are the times when you should definitely always say no? (mention what has been said in class, but also other examples).
4. What did Jesus say about yes and no?

   Are you obligated to give reasons for saying no? Yes/no, why?

   What will happen if you learn to say no when necessary? What can we learn from the character of Nehemiah and Dietrich Bonhoeffer?

Phrases to Memorize

1. Those who do not know God will make you offers to do wrong, but you must be prepared to say <u>no</u>.
2. No one can force you to say yes, so you must say <u>no</u> to everything bad, to every sin, and to everything that is not convenient in your Christian life.
3. No one can force you to say yes, so you must say <u>no</u> to everything bad, to every sin, and to everything that is not convenient in your Christian life.
4. You must always be aware of your limits, of what you can do and what is beyond your strength.
5. God has not given us a spirit of fear, but of power, love and self-control (2 Tim. 1:7).

Other Bible passages on the theme for reading and memorization

Mt. 5:37; 1 Cor. 10:13; 2 Ti. 1:7; Mt. 10:28; Is. 41:10; Mt. 6:33; Dt. 19:14; Gal. 6:5; 2 Cor. 6:14; Prov. 25:17; 1 Jn. 2:15-17; Heb. 4:15; Jn. 10:10; Prov. 29:15; Heb. 13:6; Gal. 1:10; Ps. 118:8.

55

Be a Good Leader

Memorize

Psalms 112:5 "Good will come to those who are generous and lend freely, who conduct their affairs with justice."

You are now preparing yourself for what God has in store for you when you are an adult. God may have given you leadership qualities or you may acquire them later, but you should know that a good Christian leader has a very special behavior and way of thinking. If you are a man, one day you will be the leader of a family, so pay close attention.

❓ Introductory Questions

1. How do you define a leader? Are there leaders in your school? Tell us about them.
2. Do you consider yourself a leader? What makes you a good leader?
3. What made Jesus a good leader?

Bible Story (John 13:1-20)

Being the leader of a group or your family (when you get married, if you are a man) does not mean that you can be arrogant and think you are superior to others, nor that you will be sitting on a throne giving orders, nor that you can demand and shout and force others to do what you want. Rather, being a Christian leader means that you love others, you serve them without expecting anything, you teach them Christian values, you take their opinions into account and you seek their good and growth in every way. The father, for example, should make family decisions taking into account the advice of the mother, and both will work so that their children grow strong and healthy in all aspects. The father respects the will of the mother, and both are the ones who have authority over the children. The mother recognizes that the father has authority over her; but the father loves the mother, respects her and does not force her to do anything, but serves her and treats her with delicacy.

We see what I just said in Jesus' leadership. He even served his disciples by washing their feet (something that only slaves did). The disciples followed and obeyed Jesus, but He did not impose anything on them, nor did He control them, nor repress them, nor manipulate them, nor bully them. No. The Lord listened to them, gave them freedom, treated them fairly, and maintained open communication with them. That is the kind of leader you should be. There are women who are excellent leaders, but, even if she is a leader elsewhere, in the family, because of the Lord's order, she should recognize her husband as the leader of the family. The leader has the obedience of his followers, but he is responsible for protecting them, leading them safely to a good place, and nurturing or feeding them.

Illustration

Christian leader Jean Vanier, founder of the international L'Arche community, is known worldwide for dedicating his life to promoting acceptance and care for people with mental disabilities.

On one occasion, a severely disabled man was admitted to one of the L'Arche homes. This man, let's call him Pedro, had difficulty communicating and adjusting to the new place. For weeks, Pedro was angry and frustrated, and those working at L'Arche no longer had the patience to deal with him. However, Jean Vanier, being an empathetic leader with great emotional intelligence, decided to spend time personally with Pedro. They lived together for many hours, sharing meals together, walking and talking. Jean showed such patience and unconditional love for Pedro —seeing him beyond his physical and mental limitations— that he was able to adapt to the community and feel accepted at L'Arche.

Throughout his life, Jean Vanier managed to help many people individually, inspiring others to practice compassion and respect for all human beings, regardless of their abilities or limitations.

❓ Questions About the Class

1. What is it that a good leader is not or does not do?
2. Does a good leader manipulate, mistreat, or force others to obey? Yes/no, why?
3. Tell me some things that make a father a good leader in his home.
4. Speaking of leadership, what should be the behavior of the mother with the father?
5. Why is the story of Jesus, seen in class, an example of being a good leader?
6. What is the privilege and responsibility of a good leader?
7. What were some of the leadership qualities that Jean Vanier showed?

Phrases to Memorize

1. Women can be leaders everywhere, but in the family, God has established that the leader will be the man.
2. A good leader does not believe he/she is greater than others, does not demand obedience, does not control, does not manipulate or force others to do what he/she wants.
3. The father must make decisions for the family together with the mother, respect her feelings and opinions, and love her.
4. The good leader shows humility, understands and respects the feelings and will of others, like Jesus.
5. The privilege of the leader is that his/her followers obey him/her, but his/her responsibility is to protect, guide to a good place and nourish his/her followers.

Other Bible passages on the theme for reading and memorization

Tit. 1:7-14; Prov. 16:9; 2 Cor. 8:8; Phil. 1:8-9; Mk. 10:42-45; Heb. 13:7; Gal. 6:9; Mat. 23:11; Prov. 11:14; Is. 41:10; Acts. 20:23; Prov. 29:11; Mt. 5:37; Ps. 78:72.

56

Video Games

Memorize

1 Corinthians 6:12 "'I have the right to do anything,' you say —but not everything is beneficial. 'I have the right to do anything' —but I will not be mastered by anything."

The Bible was finished writing almost two thousand years ago, so it is natural that it does not mention anything regarding video games. However, the Bible does speak to us of the ideas that should guide our lives. In this lesson, you will learn what God's will is regarding the subject of video games.

❓ Introductory Questions

1. Do you think that video games make you happy, and you can't be happy without playing them?
2. Do video games bring you closer to God or help you develop your intelligence?
3. How many of the children you know at your school are addicted to video games?

Bible Story (Matthew 17:1-8)

Obedience to God has never been boring. God created the human being and gave him the ability to imagine and be creative. However, the world always wants to make you feel that if you don't do what they do and consume what they consume, you will be a boring person, but this is a lie from Satan. The Christian life is wonderful and very exciting!

You, as a boy or girl, need to have time to play, but you must learn to manage your time. You can play a sport, participate in various activities, and have fun playing; but remember, a Christian like you knows that <u>the most important</u> thing in life is to find ways to get to know Jesus better. So, be careful, because video games are very addictive, and can cause mental disorders.

The Lord's disciples had a very exciting life following Jesus. When Jesus took Peter, James, and John aside and the four of them went up a mountain, the Bible says that Jesus' face became as bright as the sun and his clothes became as white as light. Can you imagine? Then they heard the voice of God from heaven; that was the real thing! The disciples were so excited seeing and hearing these things that they did not want to leave. You too, when you seek the Lord with all your heart, the Lord will give you real and very exciting experiences that you will never forget, and video games cannot even compare to them, because they are just a passing illusion.

Illustration

When I was in seminary, another fellow student and I were sent to a church to serve for a week. The pastor was a very kind person, and every morning we were there, he would take us into his office and spend a few minutes teaching us something. One of those days he told us that we should pray as much as possible, but he added, "I, to be honest, don't spend much time praying, because, as a pastor, I'm very busy." Do you think this pastor was right about this? Of course not! A pastor should pray even more than a non-pastor.

However, this pastor, as I have already said, was very kind. He told me to come into his office whenever I needed to. If I wanted to call my family, for example, I could pick up the phone, and without having to ask permission or knock on the door, I could use the phone that was in the office. One day, I took the liberty of going into his office to make a call to my parents and he was there. This gave me peace of mind. But when I walked in, I caught him playing a video game! There was the pastor, the one who had no time to pray!

Although there are some video games that are not bad, there are others that are very harmful because they contain violence or sex. And what's worse, they are usually addictive, and they steal valuable time from us, time that we could use to be in the presence of God. You must be very careful!

Questions About the Class

1. What are the games that help you develop your intelligence and exercise your body?
2. Why is walking with Jesus the most exciting thing in life?
3. What was one of the most exciting experiences that three of Jesus' apostles (mentioned in this lesson) had?
4. What did Peter, James, and John see and hear?
5. Why can video games be very harmful?
6. Why was the pastor in the illustration wrong in his way of thinking?

Phrases to Memorize

1. Many video games are dangerous because of their harmful content.
2. You should have time to play, but you should make sure that during your time to play you develop your imagination and your physical abilities.
3. Life is not just about playing; you should have limits for your time to play and invest enough time in seeking God —first of all— and in fulfilling your responsibilities.
4. If you seek God, the Lord will give you very exciting experiences that you can live here, and He will give you eternal life.
5. God commands us to be intelligent in the management of time.

Other Bible passages on the theme for reading and memorization

Ps. 11:5; Phil. 4:8; Eph. 5:15-17; 1 Cor. 6:12; 1 Cor. 10:23; Ps. 101:3; 2 Ti. 5:22; Lk. 12:33-34; Ps. 119:37; Eph. 5:11; Ps. 90:12; Col. 3:23-24

Note: There are video games that promote Christian values. You can ask Google or ChatGPT to inform you about them, but discuss them with your parents and church teachers.

Part VI. Relationships with Others

57

The design of family

Memorize

Psalms 133:1 "Behold, how Good and how pleasant it is for brethren to dwell together in unity!"

The family was created by God so that human beings could be happy. Does it make you happy to belong to a family? A family begins when a man and a woman join in marriage, when they get married. Then, they have the blessing of having children. You are the blessing that God gave to your family, did you know that? Parents are the authority in the family, and they, being Christians, must teach you the Word of God and to love Jesus. Also, the father is the leader of the marriage and the family. He must provide for the needs of the home, and the mother is the one who helps keep the family united and strong.

❓ Introductory Questions

1. How do you think the devil tries to destroy families?
2. Why does he want to destroy them?
3. How do you imagine your future family?
4. Do you think there are cases in which God's plan for the family should not be followed? Yes/no, why?

Bible Story (Luke 2:47-51)

The answer to the last question is no. Because God's design for family is something that will always continue until the end of human life on earth, God's Word is forever. What God has designed for us is always the best and if anyone does his own will he will suffer the consequences.

The best example we can have of the design of a family is the family of Jesus. In Jesus' family (although Jesus was the son of God, not the son of Joseph), Jesus was under the authority of His parents. Mary, his mother, was under the authority of Joseph, and Joseph was the leader of the family. Jesus loved his brothers (he had four brothers, Mary and Joseph's children), and although his brothers did not believe in Him as the Son of God at first, later, after His death and resurrection, at least two did (James and Judas) believed. Jesus' family was a very close-knit family.

Illustration

The family is the foundation that supports the entire society of a country. A highly respected magazine in the United States (US News & World Report) when studying millionaires in the United States, found that the typical image of a millionaire was a person who had worked eight to ten hours for thirty years, and was still married to the same woman. In another study of 1,365 company vice presidents, it was discovered that 87% were still married to the same woman and 92% grew up in families with a father and a mother. This means that, if you have the privilege of having a father and a mother, and they are Christians, you have the greatest treasure in the world, and great possibilities of being a very successful person. However, if this is not the case, you should have as a goal in your life to create a family according to God's design.

Questions About the Class

1. Can you tell me what God's design is for the family?
2. What is the role of children, father, and mother in the family?
3. How many siblings did Jesus have?
4. Who are Jesus' siblings that the Bible says believed in Him?
5. What did U.S. News & World Report find when it studied millionaires?
6. What is the blessing you have if you have a father and a mother and are in a Christian family? What if not?

Phrases to Memorize

1. God has designed the family in the following way: dad and mom (man and woman) and children. The children obey their parents, and the leader of the family is the father.
2. In the family, everyone has to fulfill their responsibilities and enjoy their privileges.
3. Having children is the greatest blessing of the family.
4. The devil always wants to destroy the family, so the family always has to be very united.
5. Everyone in the family helps each other, prays together, and loves each other.
6. The mother is the one who helps keep the family strong and makes it stronger.

Other Bible passages on the theme for reading and memorization

Col. 3:18-21; Prov. 18:22; Eph. 6:2-3; Eph. 5:25; Exo. 20:12; Is. 66:13; Prov. 6:20; Prov. 11:29; Prov. 14:1; Prov. 22:6; Col. 3:13; 1 Cor. 13:13; Ps. 133:1.

58

Respect for the Elderly

Memorize

Romans 13:7 "Give to everyone what you owe them: if you owe taxes, pay taxes; if revenue, then revenue; if respect, then respect; if honor, then honor."

The definition of an elder today is associated with being weak, dependent, and over 60 years old. However, not everyone over 60 is like that. In the Word of God, an elder is not someone despicable, but quite the opposite, a person worthy of honor. In fact, one of the names of God himself in the Bible is Ancient of Days (Dan. 7:9). The Bible also speaks of 24 elders who are close to God (Rev. 4:4). According to your own culture, you should show respect to those who are older than you. What expressions of respect exist in your culture towards the elderly?

❓ Introductory Questions

1. What titles are used in your culture for people older than you?
2. Who are the older people you admire the most? Why do you admire them?
3. Why do you think we should respect them?

Bible Story (2 Samuel 19:30-40)

In the Bible, only someone who has diminished physical and mental abilities is called an *elder* (physically), and before that —regardless of their age— they were called "man" or "woman," so you must be very careful in using that word. But the special respect I am talking about here is directed to all people who are older than you.

Some look down on and mock the elderly because their physical strength and mental abilities have diminished, but you must be kind and respectful to them. This includes smiling sincerely at them, raising your hand when you want to ask a question, always saying *please* when you ask for something and *thank you* when you receive it, etc. You must help them with whatever they need and recognize that we are indebted to them. We respect those who are older than us because they have more experience, and life experience brings wisdom. The older people most worthy of respect are those who have walked with the Lord for many years and those who teach and preach the Word of God.

David himself, who was the king of Israel, gave honor to Barzillai. Barzillai was an eighty-year-old man, whom the king invited to eat with him at his table. The king invited him to live with him in the palace in Jerusalem and to enjoy all that he enjoyed as king of Israel; however, Barzillai did not want to go with him, rather Barzillai wanted to continue with his own business and die in his own city.

Illustration

Fauja Singh is a retired marathon runner who is currently 113 years old [2024]. He was born in India on April 1, 1911. When he was born, he was a very weak baby and could not walk until he was five, his little legs were very thin and fragile. As a young man, he enjoyed running, but never did it professionally. It was not until he went through two tragedies, the death of his son and his wife, that he decided to run a marathon. Having immigrated to England in the 90s, he set himself the goal of running his first marathon, despite the fact that he was already 85 years old at the time; however, he managed to run it when he was 89 (in 2000). Since then, Fauja Singh continued to run marathons and retired in 2013, at the age of 102.

Fauna Singh's life inspires us to be respectful towards people who are older than us, as they can do much more than we can imagine. It also teaches us that it is not society that determines when you will be an old man, but you yourself.

The Christian life is like a marathon, and the runners with more experience always have something useful to tell us. Never look down on your elders, but rather respect and love them.

Questions About the Class

1. What are the ways to show respect to those older than you?
2. Should you call everyone older than you "elder"? Yes/no, why?
3. At what age does the Bible start calling a person "elder"?
4. What was David's behavior with the elder Berzillai?
5. What does Fauna Singh's life inspire us to do?
6. How is a marathon like the Christian life?

Phrases to Memorize

1. We must respect and honor people who are older than us.
2. We must respect more those who have had a life worthy of imitation, who have been good Christians, and even more those who work in preaching and teaching the Word of God.
3. Even those who are older and have decided to live a life of sin and whose lives are not worthy of imitation must be respected, just because they are older people.
4. Respecting and loving your elders does not imply that you have friendship with them or that you follow their advice. Your parents are the ones who determine who you can hang out with.
5. We must respect the elderly because one day we hope to be elderly too, and what we sow now, we will reap one day.

Other Bible passages on the theme for reading and memorization

Lev. 19:32; 1 Pet. 5:1; 1 Ti. 5.1; Prov. 20.29; Exo. 20:12; 1 Pet. 5:5; 1 Ti, 5:1-2; Prov. 23:22; Prov. 16:31; Mt. 15:4; Prov. 19:20; 1 Ti. 5:17-19; Job 12:12; Rom. 13:7; Job 32:4; Lam. 5:12.

59

Babies are a Blessing

Memorize

Psalms 127:3 "Lo, children are a heritage of the LORD; and the fruit of the womb is his reward."

God's wisdom will always be higher than that of human beings, because human beings are creatures, and He is the Creator. He knows everything. Every time you hear an idea that is contrary to what God says, that idea is useless, because no one can be wiser than God. The Bible says that having children is a blessing, and that the more children you have, the greater the blessing. Today many say that having many children is not good, and that we have to adapt the Bible to today's society, but rather it should be the opposite, because the Word of the Lord remains forever (Isaiah 40: 8) and the human being only for a moment (Psalms 103:15).

❓ Introductory Questions

1. How many children would you like to have when you get married? Why did you think of that number?
2. How are you preparing yourself to be a good parent to those children?
3. Why do you think having babies is a blessing from God?

Bible Story (1 Samuel 1:1-28; 2:21)

The first Book of Samuel begins by telling the story of Hannah. Hannah was a woman who for a long time was unable to have children, and although she enjoyed the love of her husband, she was not happy. One day, while praying before God, she promised the Lord that if He gave her a son, she would dedicate him to His service. Eli — the priest who ministered in those days—, judged her. Do you remember that we should not judge others? He thought she was drunk, however, he was far from the truth: she prayed and cried abundantly in the presence of God, although she prayed in silence.

God heard Hannah's prayer, and she gave birth to a son, and she named him Samuel. Samuel became a great prophet of God. However, the story does not end there. Hannah kept her promise, dedicated her child to the Lord, and He blessed her with five more children. The Bible says: "Then Eli blessed Elkanah and his wife, and said, 'The Lord give you children by this woman instead of the one she asked of the Lord.' So, they returned to their home. And the Lord visited Hannah, and she conceived and bore three sons and two daughters" (1 Samuel 2:20-21). This passage is an example of how, for God, children are a great blessing.

Illustration

The Wesley family was far from being considered a very wealthy family. Susanna married her husband Samuel when she was 19, and had 19 babies. In those days (more than three hundred years ago), medical science was not very advanced and from those 19 babies, only ten survived.

The Wesley family suffered from illness, poverty, the death of children, and twice their house burned down. But Susanna determined to be an excellent mother despite all obstacles. She was able to devote time to each of her children and teach them all to read before they were six years old. She taught them good manners, how to eat properly, and above all, to be good Christians. Susanna made it her mission to spend an hour a week with each child and teach them individually. The fruit of her labor was great: her children won hundreds of souls for the kingdom of God. Do you think Susanna fulfilled God's design for her as a woman? Do you think her children would have been what they were if she had followed the ideas of many women today?

Questions About the Class

1. Why was Hannah sad?
2. How did God bless Hannah after she consecrated her first son to God?
3. How did Eli judge Hannah?
4. What does the Bible Story teach us?
5. What can you say to a family that says they don't have time or money for children using the example of the Wesley family?
6. What did Susanna Wesley set out to do?

Phrases to Memorize

1. The world says that children are a burden, but God says that they are a blessing, and God is always right.
2. In a family, the education of children is the most important thing, so that each one of them learns to love Jesus and serve Him wholeheartedly.
3. From now on, you can begin to pray for your future family and that the Lord will give you the children He wants.
4. Raising a family properly takes a lot of effort, but in time it will give good results.

Other Bible passages on the theme for reading and memorization

Ps. 127:3-5; Prov. 17:6; Ps. 139:13-16; Gn. 1:28; Ps. 113:9; Mt. 19:14; Jer. 1:5; 1 Ti. 2:15; Mt. 18:10; 1 Ti. 5:14; Lk. 1:42; Ps. 128:3-4; 1 Chr. 26:4-5; Gn. 30:2.

60

Adoption

Memorize

Esther 2:7 "He was bringing up Hadassah, that is Esther, the daughter of his uncle, for she had neither father nor mother. The young woman had a beautiful figure and lovely to look at, and when her father and her mother died, Mordecai took her as his own daughter."

God has provided a solution for special situations where biological parents cannot care for their children, either because they have died or because they were not capable of raising them. God's solution is adoption. It is always sad when a child has no one to care for him or her, but it is a reason for great joy when he or she has an adoptive family. When he or she has an adoptive family, this family loves him/her, accepts him/her, and takes care of him/her. We must always understand that those who are adopted are exactly the same as those who are not, and in Christ, we are all adopted children.

Introductory Questions

1. What are the differences between an adopted child and a natural child?
2. Should an adopted child think that he/she does not have the same rights as natural children? Yes/no, why?
3. Why do you think God adopted us as his children? Did you know that all of God's children are adopted children?

Bible Story (Exodus 2:1-10)

In the Bible we have several cases of adoption, and among them, the first is the case of Moses. It all began with an edict from Pharaoh, king of Egypt, who ordered the killing of all children under two years old in the country. Moses was a beautiful baby, who had been born into a Jewish family, but he had to die. However, his mother could not keep him with her and decided to give him up for adoption. When a baby is given up for adoption, it does not mean that his natural parents do not love him, but that there is a situation that forced them to give him up for adoption, as in the case of Moses' parents.

When we read the story, we see that it was Pharaoh's daughter who adopted Moses, and she loved him as her own. Because belonging to a family does not depend only on blood or whether you resemble your family, but on love. The Bible always speaks positively about adoption, so much so that there was one who was also an adopted son. Do you know who it was? Jesus! Yes, Jesus was also an adopted son! Because Joseph was not his biological father (since he was conceived by the Holy Spirit), but Joseph adopted Him as his natural son. In the same way, all of us who have believed in Jesus are adopted children of his Father. Adopted children have exactly the same privileges and responsibilities as biological children. If you are an adopted child, you have two families that love you, the biological one and the one that takes care of you.

Illustration

One of the most famous and inspiring people in history is undoubtedly Steve Jobs. Steve Jobs was the founder of Apple Inc. (the company that makes computers, cell phones, etc. How would our world be today if it weren't for this man? Jobs was so smart, that he invented and improved many of the things that almost all of us use every day. Apple phones, computers, tablets, etc. Steve was born in 1955 and was the son of Joanne Carole Schieble, but being a single mother, and only 22 years old, while pregnant, she decided to give her son up for adoption. His adoptive parents were Paul and Clara Jobs. Always remember this, it is not only blood that makes us children but the love that adoptive parents have for us.

Questions About the Class

1. What was the first case of an adopted son in the Bible? Who was Moses?
2. Why was Moses adopted? Did his biological parents love Moses?
3. What is the most important case of an adopted son in the Bible?
4. What makes you belong in a family?
5. Who was Steve Jobs? What makes Steve Jobs an inspiring person?
6. Why did Steve's mother give her son up for adoption? Did Steve's biological mother love her son? Did his adoptive parents love him?

Phrases to Memorize

1. Being an adopted child gives you exactly the same privileges and responsibilities as a biological child.
2. The examples of the Bible and of Steve Jobs and others show that being an adopted child does not stop God from planning your life in any way.
3. You should always feel loved because your biological parents love you and if you are an adopted child, your adoptive parents do too.
4. We are all adopted children of God.

Other Bible passages on the theme for reading and memorization

Jas. 1:27; Mt. 18:5; Is. 1:17; Prov. 31:8; Eph. 1:5; Ps. 146:9; Mt. 25:40; Acts. 7:21; Gal. 4:5-7; Rom. 9:8; Est. 2:7; Gal. 3:26; Jn. 14:18.

61

Our Friends

Memorize

Proverbs 13:20 "Whoever walks with the wise becomes wise, but the companion of fools will suffer harm."

We all need to have friends, and although God commands us to love all people, we are free to choose our friends. Therefore, we have to be very wise in choosing who to hang out with, because the Bible says: "He who walks with wise men will be wise..." Likewise, it also says: "Bad conversations corrupt good morals" (1 Cor. 15:33). This means that if you hang out with bad people and with bad habits, you will soon be doing and saying the same things as them.

❓ Introductory Questions

1. How many friends do you have? What are their names? What are they like?
2. What do you look for when choosing your friends?
3. How would you describe a good friend?
4. Do you think that the friends you have really value your friendship? Yes/no, why?

Bible Story (Job 2:11-13)

A true friend loves at all times and shows that love with Acts; his/her company brings joy; he/she knows how to give wise and affectionate advice, but also reprimands when necessary. He or she speaks well of others and knows how to keep personal information safe.

There are different levels of friendship. It ranges from a casual friendship (we can talk to that person once a year, for example) to an intimate friendship (often). We should never choose as a close friend a person who does not know God or who is not a good person. Sometimes it is difficult to find a good Christian at school, or later, when you are an adult, at work; however, you should at least hang out with those people who you observe do not swear or behave badly. You should never hang out with someone who talks about sex or steals or lies or cheats others. You can be friendly with them, but you cannot make these people close friends.

Job was a very good Christian. He lived in a time when the Bible did not yet exist, thousands of years before you and I were born. Job had three friends, who, when they found out what was happening to him, went to visit him... By the way, do you know Job's story? Well, they decided to visit him, and that was good, but if you continue reading what they said, you will realize that, instead of comforting and encouraging him, they condemned him. A good friend would never do that, because they could not know why this was happening to Job. What would you have done if you had been a friend of Job and had seen his situation?

Illustration

The people you hang out with, whether you want to or not, shape your character. You decide who you hang out with, but it is also natural. This means that if you are a good Christian, you will also tend to hang out with good Christians. However, you must be careful, because there are people who appear to be Christians, but are not. Your parents will always be good counselors in this matter, so you should talk to them about the people you hang out with. On the other hand, try not to be antisocial, but talk to everyone, talk to them about the Lord and invite them to church. But remember, you must always be very careful in choosing who you will have a *close* friendship with.

On one occasion a farmer took out his shotgun and went into his field to shoot at a flock of very annoying and harmful crows. He fired several shots and went to see who he had hit. When he went to look, the farmer was surprised to see a parrot, very friendly, but now dead. When the farmer's son came to see too, he asked his father: "What happened, dad?" "Bad company," the father replied.

If we hang out with the wrong people, they can get us into serious trouble and suffer unnecessarily.

Questions About the Class

1. Is it important to have friends? Yes/No, why?
2. If God commands us to love everyone, are we obliged to have the wrong friends? Yes/No, why?
3. Can you mention some characteristics of a good friend?
4. What kind of friend should we never have?
5. Why did Job's friends prove to be not really good friends?
6. Who should you always tell who you are hanging out with?
7. Why did the parrot do what it did?

Phrases to Memorize

1. We should always choose good Christians as our best friends.
2. Your parents should always know who you hang out with (and what they are like).
3. A good friend treats you as he would treat himself. He behaves like a Christian and speaks words that make you grow in Christ. He is a helper and lets you help him too.
4. You should stay away from someone who talks about sex or steals or is rude to his parents or cheats others, etc. Those who do not love Jesus cannot be your close friends.
5. You should pray for God to give you good friends. And the person you marry one day, that person will be your best friend.

Other Bible passages on the theme for reading and memorization

Prov. 18:24; Jn. 15:13; Prov. 27:17; Prov. 17:17; Ecc. 4:9-12; 1 Cor. 15:33; 1 Ts. 5:11; Prov. 27:9; Prov. 27:6; Job 6:14; Prov. 13:20.

62

Compassion for Others

Memorize

Matthew 7:12 "Therefore all things whatsoever ye would that men should do to you, do ye even so to them: for this is the law and the prophets."

This verse from Matthew 7:12 has been called the *golden rule*. There are many people in the world who are suffering right now. You may not know it, but people cry and suffer at this precise moment. A person may be suffering because of his/her own sins; but there are also many who are suffering because of the sins of others. Many times we will never know exactly why a person is suffering. Fortunately, the Lord has not commanded us to investigate why a person is suffering or to judge him/her. He only wants us to help him/her and have compassion on him/her.

Introductory Questions

1. If you hear about someone who is suffering, who do you think of first?
2. How could you help an orphan child or an old woman who has lost her husband?
3. Is there a poor boy/girl at your school who other children make fun of? Have you defended him/her?
4. Have you ever been in an orphanage? If so, tell us about your experience.

Bible Story (Luke 10:30-35)

Jesus once told a story to illustrate loving one's neighbor. Many people think they should be good and help those who do good to them and help them. And while this is true, the Lord commands us to help all those we have the opportunity to, including strangers. We need to show compassion for others who are suffering. The word *compassion* means "to suffer with." That is, we should put ourselves in the shoes of the person who is suffering and help him/her.

The story that Jesus told is about a man who was attacked by robbers, who left him naked and badly wounded. First, a priest passed by, a religious man who taught the law of God, but he ignored him and passed by on the other side. Then another priest passed by, a Levite, that is, a person who served in the church, but he also passed by on the other side. Finally, one who was considered an enemy of the Jews, a Samaritan, passed by; and he had compassion on the man on the ground. He put him on his own horse, healed him, and took him to the nearest hospital to be cared for.

This story teaches us that every Christian should have compassion for those who are suffering and should treat them as he or she would like to be treated if he or she were in their place.

Illustration

D.L. Moody was an evangelist who won many souls to Christ. He had tremendous compassion for others and cared for them in order to save them from the clutches of hell. In his book *A History of American Revivals*, Frank Grenville Beardsley tells the story of his conversion. He says that Moody said that when he was a boy, his Sunday School teacher came to the counter of the store where he worked, put his hand on his shoulder, and began to talk to him about Christ. As he talked, the Sunday School teacher was shedding tears. "There was this man," D.L. Moody continued, "shedding tears for my sins, when I had not shed a single tear for them myself. This was a sign of great compassion for me."

This story teaches us that the greatest show of compassion we can have for a person is to speak to them about the Lord to help them escape from hell, the great condemnation that Jesus and the apostles spoke of. We are naturally selfish and do not think of others, but the Holy Spirit is the one who helps us develop a spirit of compassion for others.

Questions About the Class

1. What is the verse from Matthew 7:12 called? Can you recite it from memory?
2. According to this lesson, what has God called us to? What has He not called us to?
3. Should we only help those who do good to us? Yes/No, why?
4. What does the word *compassion* mean?
5. What do you think of the priest and the Levite who passed by and did not help the man who was lying on the ground?
6. What do you think of the Samaritan who helped his neighbor?
7. What was D.L. Moody's conversion like? What does this story teach us?

Phrases to Memorize

1. We must ask the Lord to send us the Holy Spirit to have compassion for those who suffer.
2. Having compassion is not only about having a feeling of pity, but acting as if you were going through that suffering and helping others.
3. God commands not only to help those who help you, but to help everyone, including those who treat you badly and strangers.
4. In every situation you must apply the golden rule (what you want done to you, you must also do to others).
5. The greatest demonstration of compassion for others is to help them be saved. Jesus had compassion on us and He wants us to have compassion on others.

Other Bible passages on the theme for reading and memorization

Eph. 4:32; Col. 3:12; Gal. 6:2; 1 Pet. 3:8; Mt. 7:12; Gal. 5:22-23; Mt. 9:36-38; 1 Jn. 3:17; Zac. 7:8-10; Ps. 86:15; 2 Cor. 1:3-4; Job 19:21; Is. 54:8; Rom. 10:1; Rom. 9:3.

63

Grandparents

Memorize

2 Timothy 1:5 "I am reminded of your sincere faith, a faith that dwelt first in your grandmother Lois and your mother Eunice and now, I am sure, dwells in you as well."

Not all of us have or have had the privilege of having Christian grandparents. But it is God's will that you, one day, be a Christian grandparent who teaches your children and grandchildren to serve the Lord. God's will is that the teachings of the gospel be taught from generation to generation, and God often uses grandparents in this very important task. The evil society in which we live today has no respect for grandparents or the elderly (as we saw in a previous class); but if you have the privilege of having a Christian grandparent, you should be very attentive to him/her and learn from him/her. If they are Christians and your parents are too, you should consider this as an enormous blessing.

Introductory Questions

1. Are your grandparents Christians? If not, have you talked to them about Jesus? And if they are, do they teach you about the Word of God?
2. What do you most admire in your grandparents?
3. Why should you treat your grandparents with love and respect?

Bible Story (Gn. 48:1-22)

Joseph had been sold by his brothers and ended up in the land of Egypt. There God exalted Joseph and made him the second most important man in the country. When this happened, God made it possible for him to bring his family to Egypt. Jacob, his father, was a very wise man, a servant of God. When Jacob recognized Joseph, he asked about his children. Joseph had married in Egypt and had two sons, Ephraim and Manasseh. Jacob then recognized a problem: these children lacked a Christian education; that is why he told Joseph that these children would be his. Jacob adopted them as his own and blessed them.

Have you noticed that there are lists of people's names in the Bible? These lists of names are called genealogies. Do you know why these genealogies are in the Bible? The reason for this is that God wants human beings to serve Him from generation to generation. That should be your desire as well.

Illustration

Grandparents are very important in strengthening the family. When they were children, they looked like you physically. By the way, how are you like them? But also (and this is the most important thing) they transmit values and teachings. When grandparents are Christians, they pray for their family and pass on the torch of the fear of God to their children and grandchildren. Perhaps you are one of them.

In the Bible we have the story of Ruth. Why is this story in the Bible? Because of Obed, because Obed was David's grandfather, and Jesus was a descendant of David. One of your greatest desires should be that you become the grandfather of a great man of God or a great woman of God.

You may have heard of Martin Luther King Jr. He was a civil rights leader in the United States, fought to make the country free from discrimination, and is considered a national hero. He also won the Nobel Peace Prize in 1964. However, before being a politician, he considered himself, above all, a Baptist preacher. He said, "This is my being and my heritage," he once said, "because I am also the son of a Baptist preacher, the grandson of a Baptist preacher, and the great-grandson of a Baptist preacher."

❓ Questions About the Class

1. According to what we studied in this lesson, what is God's will?
2. What was the problem that Jacob recognized in his grandchildren (the sons of Joseph)?
3. What is the reason for genealogies in the Bible?
4. What is the most important function of Christian grandparents?
5. Why is the Book of Ruth so important in the Bible?
6. Who was Martin Luther King Jr.?
7. What did Martin Luther King Jr. consider to be his greatest legacy?

Phrases to Memorize

1. God's will is that the flame of the gospel be kept alive from generation to generation in your family.
2. If your parents and grandparents are Christians, consider this a great privilege. If they are not, pray to God to save them.
3. The reason genealogies appear in the Bible is to honor the generation of good and God-fearing people throughout history.
4. The most important function of grandparents is to give Christian counsel and teaching of the Word of God to their children and grandchildren.

Other Bible passages on the theme for reading and memorization

Prov. 17:6; Prov. 16:31; Ps. 145:4; Dt. 4:9; Prov. 13:22; 2 Ti. 1:5; Ps. 103:17; Is. 46:4; Ps. 37:25; Ps. 90:12, 14; Exo. 10:2; Ps. 72:5; Ps. 79:13; Ps. 89:1; Ps. 90:1; Ps. 135:13.

64

The Power of Your Tongue

Memorize

Proverbs 18:21 "Death and life are in the power of the tongue, and those who love it will eat its fruits."

Jesus said that the tree is known by its fruit and this fruit consists of our words and actions. He also said that out of what the heart is full, so the mouth speaks. The Christian must fill his or her heart with the words of God (words of faith and wisdom) and ask the Holy Spirit to help him/her so that those words become part of him/her. The apostle Paul also said that the Word of Christ dwells in us richly (Col. 3:16). If we manage to make our words the right words, we will please God and others. By our words we will be found righteous and by our words guilty (Mt. 12:37). Our sincere words are, one could say, the most important thing about us.

Introductory Questions

1. Do you remember any words that encouraged you to keep going?
2. What is the topic you talk about most during the day?
3. What are you doing to speak like Jesus spoke?

Bible Story (Matthew 15:21-28; Mark 7:24-30)

On one occasion Jesus went to a region of Tyre and Sidon and entered a house; and although He did not want anyone to know about it, He could not hide. A foreign woman came to Him to beg the Lord to cast a demon out of her daughter. But the Lord told her something that she perhaps did not expect: the Lord tested her by telling her that He was sent only to the Israelites and not to foreigners, and He even gave her a somewhat humiliating illustration: "Let the children be satisfied first, for it is not right to take the children's bread and throw it to the dogs." However, she was a humble woman, and she answered: "Yes, Lord; but even the dogs under the table eat the children's crumbs." Her words were words of humility and faith. Therefore, Jesus said to her: "Because of this word, go; the demon has left your daughter." God considers our words to be very important.

Illustration

In 1775, in the state of Virginia, Patrick Henry gave a speech known as "Liberty or Death." This was a very inspiring speech that transformed the course of human history. This speech encouraged the inhabitants of the American colonies to take up arms and fight for their independence from England. Among the words of his speech, Patrick shouted: "Give me liberty or give me death!" This speech convinced the colonists to fight against England. The result of this was the independence of the United States in 1776. The words have changed the course of history.

You may well remember someone who has given you a word of encouragement, but a word of discouragement can also be powerful in your life. What you say can be what lands you in jail or what gives you freedom. God gives value to your words because they will also lead you to failure or victory. Every day you must pray to God that His Holy Spirit will put the words you should speak during the day, and put His Words (the Bible) in the center of your heart.

The Facebook page Humans of Dublin posted on August 3, 2015 the story of Jamie, a teenager living in Dublin, Ireland. He rode his bike over the sidewalk of a bridge where a man was about to commit suicide. Jamie didn't know what was happening to this man, but at the exact moment he was about to jump, Jamie said, "Are you okay?" Everything that happened next was a result of those words, as this man not only regretted committing suicide, but three months later he texted Jamie that his wife would have a son and that they would name him after him, Jamie. He also told him that those three words had saved his life: "Are you okay?"

Questions About the Class

1. What did Jesus say, how do you know a tree?
2. What did Jesus say was the reason for the words we speak?
3. How can we speak God's words of faith and wisdom?
4. Why are our words so important?
5. What was the reason Jesus cast out the demon from the foreign woman?
6. What was a speech that changed the course of history? What were the three words Jamie said that saved a man's life?

Phrases to Memorize

1. You have to be very careful about what you say. One of the most important things in life is to learn to speak words of faith and wisdom always.
2. The way you can speak God's words in the Bible is by memorizing them and asking God to turn His Word into a living and powerful Word within you by the Holy Spirit.
3. The words you speak can save a person's life, but they can also cause a person's life to be lost. You yourself will be judged before God by your words.
4. Our sincere words, it can be said, are the most important thing about us.

Other Bible passages on the theme for reading and memorization

1 Pet. 3:10; Prov. 15:1-2; Eph. 4:29; Ps. 141:3; Mt. 12:36-37; Jas. 1:26; Prov. 12:18; Jas. 3:8; Prov. 15:4; Prov. 10:19; Prov. 13:3; Ps. 19:14; Jas. 3:6; Jas. 1:19; Prov. 15:28; Prov. 21:23; Phil. 2:14; Ps. 34:13; Prov. 25:15; Prov. 17:27.

65

How to Distinguish a True Christian

Memorize

Matthew 7:16 "Ye shall know them by their fruits. Do men gather grapes of thorns, or figs of thistles?"

Christ tells us not to judge, that is, to think things we don't know; but at the same time, He tells us to recognize the sheep (true Christians) from the wolves (those who pretend to be Christians). How will we know? By their fruits. The fruits are their sincere words and their actions (the decisions they make). A person can pretend for a while, but sooner or later the fruit will appear: they will say what they shouldn't and make decisions and actions that are not those of a true follower of Jesus Christ. Jesus said that these wolves are raptors, that is, they steal. A wolf will steal your peace, your valuable time, your communion with Christ, and your happiness. In this lesson I will help you identify the wolves.

Introductory Questions

1. What are the differences between a sheep and a wolf?
2. Why do you think God uses the sheep as an example of what a true Christian is?
3. What does the wolf want? Why does he go where the sheep are?

How to identify a Fake Christian

1. **False Christians are Satan's instruments to steal peace, joy, time, money, etc.**, from the Lord's sheep. The devil's goal is to lead us away from Christ and lead us to hell. On many occasions, the Lord and the apostles warned us about these people. Here I will present some ideas that will help you identify wolves. I will give the example of a wolf (clothed in sheep's clothing) trying to deceive a young Christian man or woman.

2. **His or her desires are not to serve Christ.** You can ask him or her, "What are your greatest desires?" "What do you think is your purpose in this life?" He/she may answer something like, "I would like to be an ideal husband and father, provide for my family, be loving and kind to my wife, etc." But that answer could be a sign that he/she has not yet converted to the Lord, because the truly converted will say that he/she wants to serve the Lord, that his/her greatest desire is to be useful to Him, and that his/her hope is to be with Christ for eternity. That is, spiritual things.

3. **He or she does not seek the kingdom of God first.** Those who do not yet know the Lord they love the things of this world more than the things of God; they may be hard workers or good students, but they do not put the Lord first in their life. A true Christian loves Christ and always puts Him first. If you ask such a Christian: What do you love most? What are your daily activities? He/she will tell you with all sincerity that what he/she loves most is Christ, and what he/she does during the day includes, first of all, prayer and reading the Bible.

4. **He/she does not worship.** Observe, a true Christian worships the Lord. You see him lift up his hands and shed his tears because he feels the presence of the Lord. He sings with all his heart. He likes to pray and sets aside enough time to talk to the Lord.
5. **He has no desire to talk about Christ.** The wolf does not get excited when mentioning the name of Jesus, nor does he confess Him as his personal Savior to his friends and family.
6. **His/Her family cannot testify that he/she is a true Christian.** His family may testify of his/her true conversion, but they do not see any change in him/her. When someone has truly converted to the Lord, those who live with him/her can testify of the radical change that has occurred in his/her life.
7. **Does not seek the company of Christians to be edified in Christ.** He/she seeks Christians only to benefit from material things or the things of the world, but he/she does not love to listen to the Word of God.
8. **He/she is not willing to sacrifice for Christ.** The true convert asks himself/herself: What can I sacrifice and what of my life can I use to serve my Lord? Since now, he/she belongs to Christ and is willing even to die if necessary for the Lord.
9. **He/she is not humble.** He/she who has converted to the Lord is meek and humble (like a sheep), he forgives and asks for forgiveness; he serves with humility of heart and does not think himself better than others. He also humbly submits to the authority placed by God.

Illustration

The reason the leader of a church was called by God to be a pastor is because he/she is the person who must first identify the wolves and warn the sheep. Jesus said that the way we can identify a wolf from a sheep is by its actions and words, that is, the fruit. He said that just as a tree is known by its fruit, so we would know true Christians from non-Christians. We must wait for the time when the tree will bear its fruit.

When we have identified a false Christian, we must distance ourselves from that person (see 1 Cor. 5:11). In that case, the sign that that person is truly converted is that he confesses that he previously pretended to be a Christian, but that he/she was not, and that he/she had a real encounter with the Lord Jesus.

Activity

Identify the wolf from the sheep, mark with a cross the W (for wolf) and the S (for sheep):

1. A boy who cheats in school (W) (S).
2. He always tells the truth, even if the truth seems to be against him (W) (S).
3. He admits that he is wrong and asks for forgiveness (W) (S).
4. He never asks for forgiveness or humbles himself before others (W) (S).
5. Someone who blames others for his/her mistakes (W) (S).
6. He is willing to go to great lengths to be with you, but is not willing to do the least for Jesus (W) (S).
7. He gets angry easily (W) (S).
8. He is ashamed to talk about Jesus (W) (S).
9. He is not moved or touched when he hears about Jesus' sacrifice on the cross (W) (S).
10. He does things in secret to please God (e.g., gives to the poor) without seeking to please other people (W) (S).

Questions About the Class

1. How can we identify a sheep from a wolf? What did Jesus say?
2. Mention the differences between a true Christian and someone who is not.
3. Is identifying a wolf judging? Yes/no, why?
4. How can we protect others from people we have identified as wolves? Who is mainly the one God has appointed in the church to identify wolves?
5. What should we do when identifying the wolf?
6. How could we know if a wolf has finally become a sheep?

Phrases to Memorize

1. Judging is giving an opinion of someone before knowing their actions and words. Christ commands us to observe people and wait until they bear fruit.
2. Fruit will determine whether a person is a Christian or a fake.
3. False Christians are instruments of the devil to steal our peace, time, money, and to destroy our relationship with Christ, and turn us away from Him.
4. Wolves do not think about spiritual things but always about the things of the earth. Wolves do not delight in the Lord nor do they like to pray, nor do they love the Bible.

Practical example

If you like a boy/girl and he/she is not a Christian, you must ask God to help you overcome this evil desire. You must immediately take your eyes off it, because it is a trap of the devil. You must not give it any entrance until he/she is truly converted to the Lord. The fruit is what will make you know it, and this fruit must be present for a long time (until spiritual maturity). You must be very careful, because the devil wants to ruin your life. You must always talk about it with your parents and with your pastor and his wife (or), and with them together.

Other Bible passages on the theme for reading and memorization

Lk. 10:3; Jn. 10:12; Mt. 10:16; Acts. 20:29; Exo. 22:27; 2 Pet. 2:1; 1 Pet. 5:8; 2 Cor. 11:13-15; Lk. 6:46; Mt. 7:20-23; 1 Cor. 5:11.

66

Do not Compare Yourself with Others

Memorize

2 Corinthians 10:12 "We do not dare to classify or compare ourselves with some who commend themselves. When they measure themselves by themselves and compare themselves with themselves they are not wise."

You should always think about being better before the Lord. You should seek to improve in your studies and advance in your Christian character. However, it is not healthy to compare yourself with others, because you are different from others and God has created you that way. You can have other people (mostly adults, who are still alive or who have already died) as your heroes because of their life of faith and you should imitate them, but it is not good to compare yourself with other boys/girls who are now walking with you in life, because it will not generate anything good.

❓ Introductory Questions

1. Why do you think comparing yourself to others can lead to jealousy and quarrels?
2. What do you think of those who say, "everyone does it" or "compared to that one, I am a white dove"?
3. Why does comparison produce pride in the heart?

Bible Story (Luke 18:9-14)

Jesus told the story of two men who went into the temple to pray. One was a Pharisee and the other was a tax collector (publican). In his prayer, the Pharisee compared himself to the publican and, comparing himself to the others and to the publican who was there, he said, "I thank you that I am not like other men, extortioners, unjust, adulterers, or even like this publican." Meanwhile, the publican confessed his sins before God and humbled himself before Him. Jesus said that while the publican was saved, the Pharisee would be humbled by God.

This story teaches us that we should never compare ourselves with others, but rather only be concerned with what each of us should do and do it. Comparisons with others produce various sins (greed, envy, avarice, jealousy, anger, self-contempt, etc.).

Illustration

Tony hailed a cab; the cab stopped and the driver said, "You did everything perfect, Paco." "Paco? Who's Paco?" Tony replied. "Oh, he's a guy who did everything right... an excellent tennis player and a winner of world-class shooting competitions; he was always on time, always polite, sang like a tenor, and was an artist in painting." "Like that?" Tony said admiringly. "Yes, and he remembered all the names of his extended family, their birthdays, and important dates; he earned several college degrees, and he could fix everything from cars to airplanes. Not like me, who doesn't even know how to change a fuse, and if I do, I'll knock out the power

SPIRITUAL RESILIENCE

in the whole neighborhood." "But how and where did you meet this amazing, extraordinary man?" "I never met him," the cab driver said. "I married his widow."

This story reminds us that we should not make comparisons. Every person is different and has different qualities. The design and calling that God made for your life is different from that of another, and you are a unique person in the world. Comparisons can be instruments of the enemy to lead us to sin. You should feel grateful and satisfied for who you are, and for all that you have received from God.

❓ Questions About the Class

1. Why is it unhealthy to compare yourself to others? Give me three reasons.
2. Should you have heroes and good Christians that you look up to (adults who have achieved a life of faith)? Yes/No, why?
3. What was the Pharisee saying in the Bible Story? Why did what he said not please God?
4. What does the Bible Story teach us?
5. How do you think the taxi driver felt because his wife compared him to her dead husband?
6. What does the illustration teach us?

Phrases to Memorize

1. God has created each one of us different, with different and distinct abilities, therefore, it is foolish to compare ourselves with others.
2. Comparisons make you insensitive to sin, because the devil deceives people into thinking that if they are "better" than another, then they are right before God.
3. Comparisons lead you to pride, because you may think you are "better" than someone else.
4. Comparisons limit your potential, because you may be comparing yourself with someone who has less strength or fewer abilities than you.
5. Comparisons make you ignore that everything we have and can do is because of the Lord. We have received everything from God.

Other Bible passages on the theme for reading and memorization

2 Cor. 10:12; Gal. 1:10; Gal. 6:4-5; Phil. 2:3; Mt. 7:2; 2 Cor. 3:5; 2 Ti. 2:15; Exo. 20:17; Jn. 21:22; Lk. 22:24-27; Gal. 6:3-5; Lk. 18:9-14; 1 Cor. 4:6-8; Mk. 9:23.

67

Forgive Always

Memorize

Matthew 6:14 "For if you forgive other people when they sin against you, your heavenly Father will also forgive you. But if you do not forgive others their sins, your Father will not forgive your sins."

One of the most important signs that a person follows Christ is that he always forgives. The world always classifies offenses and says that some are more serious than others, and while this is true in the sense that some offenses bring more suffering and consequences than others, none of them can compare with those suffered by Christ for us, and the Lord forgave them all on the cross. Therefore, God sets a requirement for Him to forgive us: that we forgive all offenses committed against us, no matter how serious each one is.

❓ Introductory Questions

1. What is the biggest offense you have ever received? Have you forgiven it yet?
2. What do you think is better, to forgive quickly or to take a long time to forgive? Why?
3. Why do the offenses we have received not compare to those Jesus suffered for us?

Bible Story (Matthew 8:21-35)

Peter asked the Lord how many times he should forgive his brother. He thought he should forgive him up to seven times; however, the Lord Jesus answered him no, not seven, but seventy times seven; that is 490 times; in a word, always.

Then Jesus told the story of a man who owed a billion dollars to a king. Since this man was poor, it was impossible for him to pay the debt. The king told him that if he did not pay, then he and his wife and children would have to work for free all their lives until they paid it off. The man went to the king and knelt down and begged him to be patient with him. The king, moved with mercy, forgave him everything he owed.

When this man was gone from the king's presence, he found a fellow-man of his who owed him a dollar. The latter being even poorer, he fell at the feet of the man whom the king had forgiven, and begged him with tears to be patient with him; but the other would not, and he threw his fellow-man into prison. When this happened, those who saw it told the king. And the king said to him, "Why have you done this? I forgave you a billion dollars, and you will not forgive a dollar?" Then he ordered him to be punished until he should pay all that he owed.

Illustration

Corrie Ten Boom wrote a wonderful book about her own story. She and her family were captured by the Nazi army and taken to a place where they tortured and killed Jews. While there, her sister was tortured and killed, but she miraculously survived.

Later, being a Christian, she devoted herself to preaching the forgiveness of Jesus throughout Germany and in many other countries. One day, speaking to a group of people in Munich, she was preaching that Jesus had forgiven all our sins on the cross. Among the attendees was a very familiar person to her. How could she not recognize him! He was the cruelest man she had ever met. A man who had tortured and killed many people in the place where she had been. When the talk was over, the man approached her and said: "Sister Corrie, it is wonderful to talk about forgiveness... I myself was one of those you mentioned in your talk, but now I have accepted Jesus Christ into my heart, and I know that He has forgiven me. But I would like to hear from your own lips that you have forgiven me too." Then the man extended his hand to Corrie. She was paralyzed; she had been talking about forgiveness, but now she herself was reluctant to forgive. The man did not recognize her, but she recognized him. Corrie knew who he was! So after a couple of seconds, she also shook his hand, and said with tears in her eyes: "Yes, brother, I forgive you with all my heart."

Questions About the Class

1. What is one of the most important signs of a true follower of Jesus?
2. How many times should we forgive? What does that number mean?
3. What happens if we do not forgive someone for their offense against us?
4. What did the man whose great debt the king forgave him do to his companion? What did the king do next?
5. What was Corrie's experience with the Nazis?
6. What did she say to the former Nazi soldier?

Phrases to Memorize

1. One of the most important signs that identifies a person who follows Christ is that he forgives others for their offenses.
2. Jesus forgave all our offenses against Him, therefore, He demands that we forgive all those who offend us.
3. The requirement for God to forgive our offenses is that we forgive those that others do to us.
4. The requirement for forgiveness does not depend on how serious the offense is.
5. When Jesus was asked how many times we should forgive, Jesus answered that always (seventy times seven).
6. Forgive immediately, because until you forgive, God will not forgive you either.

Other Bible passages on the theme for reading and memorization

Eph. 4:32; Mk. 11:25; 1 Jn. 1:9; Mt. 6:14-15; Mt. 18:21-22; Mt. 6:14-15; Lk. 6:37; Col. 3:13; Jas. 5:16; Lk. 6:27; Ps. 103:10-14; Prov. 10:12; Mt. 6:12.

68

If you Make a Mistake, Ask for Forgiveness At Once

Memorize

Matthew 5:25 "Settle matters quickly with your adversary who is taking you to court. Do it while you are still together on the way, or your adversary may hand you over to the judge, and the judge may hand you over to the officer, and you may be thrown into prison."

The requirement to continue having peace with God is to do everything in our power to have peace with everyone. We all could at some point (even unintentionally) offend another person, but the intelligent child and young person asks for forgiveness and apologizes immediately; and the most intelligent ones are not offended by almost anything. Jesus says that each one has a time to take advantage of and ask for forgiveness, otherwise, things will get worse and worse.

Introductory Questions

1. What offends you the most? Do you think Jesus can help you to stop being offended by it?
2. Why do you think people don't want to ask for forgiveness?
3. Do you think there are people who get offended but are not sincere and say they were not offended? Why do you think they do this?

Bible Story (Matthew 8:21-35)

The greatest demonstration of God's love is His forgiveness. And Christ, at the moment He was being seriously offended, when He was on the cross, said: "Father, forgive them, for they know not what they do" (Luke 23:24). He did not need anyone to ask for forgiveness in order to forgive; but a person, in order to make forgiveness effective, needs to ask the Lord for forgiveness (although He had already forgiven us all our sins). So too, we should not wait for someone to ask us for forgiveness in order to forgive them (because we should forgive them in our hearts as quickly as we can, the faster the better); but if we are the ones who offend, we should ask for forgiveness and apologize immediately.

The Bible says, "You shall not revile [offend] the judges, nor speak evil of [speak evil of] the prince [ruler] of your people [where you live]" (Ex. 22:28). Paul, a powerful servant of God, was taken prisoner for preaching the gospel, and he was brought before the authorities for trial. When he had a chance to speak, he said that he had served God without committing any crime. Then one of the rulers, Ananias, ordered Paul to be severely beaten on the mouth. Then he said to the man, "God will strike you, you whitewashed wall! Are you sitting to judge me by obeying the law, and do you not obey it by commanding me to be beaten?" Paul was saying the right thing, because that should not be done in a trial.

But when Paul said this, they asked him, "Are you thus offending your authority?" Paul then realized that he had made a mistake in saying this and immediately apologized.

Illustration

A London newspaper owner in the 19th century (when newspapers were a very important medium of communication), William B., badmouthed a politician (Edward H.) in his newspaper and publicly insulted him. Later, he met that same politician in the bathroom of a London club and said to him: "Edward, I want to apologize to you, I was wrong, I am sorry." The politician groaned a little and said: "Very well, William, I forgive you, but next time, I want you to insult me in the bathroom and then apologize to me in the newspaper." This story teaches us that if we insult someone publicly, we should also apologize publicly, and not in private.

Questions About the Class

1. What is the requirement that God sets for us to continue in peace with Him?
2. What does an intelligent person do when he makes a mistake and/or offends another? What do the most intelligent people do?
3. How long did it take Jesus to forgive his offenders? Did he need them to ask for forgiveness?
4. What should we do if we make a mistake and offend another person or make a mistake?
5. What did Paul do when he made a mistake? How did he make that mistake?
6. What does the illustration of this class teach us today?

Phrases to Memorize

1. Jesus tells us that if we make a mistake, we should ask for forgiveness and apologize immediately, otherwise we will have more serious problems.
2. It is normal that at some point in life we offend another person unintentionally, but we must apologize.
3. If we intentionally offend a person, we should still ask for forgiveness, and pray to God first, to achieve reconciliation.
4. A wise person is not offended by anything, and forgives immediately.
5. If we offend a person and do them harm (for example, if we damage their reputation publicly [A Christian would never do that]) we must make amends.

Other Bible passages on the theme for reading and memorization

1 Jn. 1:9; Jas. 5:16; Ps. 51:10; Mt. 18:15; Mt. 5:23-24; Prov. 6:16-19; Col. 3:13; Lk. 17:3; Gal. 6:7-8; Job 4:8; Rom. 12.18.

69

Accept People as They Are

Memorize

Romans 15:7 "Accept one another, then, just as Christ accepted you, in order to bring praise to God."

We are all different, and we are different because God made us that way. There are things you did not ask for: where you were born, your race, your nationality, your language, where you live now, your sex, your parents, your temperament, your height. God also gives certain abilities, riches, gifts, and talents to some that he does not give to others. He has created diversity. You must be the one who never discriminates against anyone for what he or she cannot change, and accepts everyone within certain limits. We will talk about this in this class.

Introductory Questions

1. How are you different from others at your school? Are there people at your school who are not from any Christian denomination? How are they treated?
2. Is there bullying at your school? Have you ever been discriminated against for any reason?
3. Why do you think it is very important for a person to be accepted?

Bible Story (John 4:7-39)

Although Christians are promoters of equality, we also know that there are limits. These limits are compliance with the law, respect for each person's own culture and that of their family, religious beliefs, the right to expression and opinion, etc. Accepting people as they are means that you must love and respect people regardless of how much they have, the ideas they have, their sex, their abilities, their disabilities, their race, skin color, religion, family status, marital status, nationality, family, surname and language. There should not be categories of people in your mind because of these things. Every person has the right to receive the gospel, the love of God, and to be treated with dignity, justice and respect.

However, no one can force you (with the excuse of not discriminating) to change your Christian identity, your family culture, to not express your ideas, to not talk about Christ, or to accept what is against your principles. Christians fight against ideas that promote sin, because sin destroys humanity (John 10:10; Rom. 6:23).

In the passage from John 4, Jesus was talking to a Samaritan woman. In those days —two thousand years ago— there was a lot of prejudice and discrimination. The Jews believed that they were superior to other races, and they believed that men were superior to women. However, Jesus treated the Samaritan woman with the same treatment and the same respect and with the same justice and dignity that he treated his male Jewish disciples.

Illustration

David Brainerd was an 18th-century Christian missionary whose life has been an inspiration to thousands of Christian leaders. He is best known for his work among the indigenous peoples of North America. With the goal of bringing the gospel to a tribe living in New Jersey —known for its distrust of European settlers— rather than imposing his beliefs, Brainerd lived among them, learning their language and customs. On one occasion, during a fierce winter, the natives became seriously ill, and although Brainerd was also ill, he dedicated his time to caring for them and gave them his meager food and medicines.

One evening, a tribal elder, touched by Brainerd's dedication and compassion, approached him and said, "Never before has a white man treated us with such respect and love." Brainerd humbly replied, "God loves us all equally, and it is my duty and honor to serve you as brothers." Brainerd never discriminated against the Indians, and in this way he had the opportunity to share Christ with them and win many souls.

Questions About the Class

1. What are at least seven things that you did not ask for and that you cannot change about yourself?
2. What are some limits to the idea of non-discrimination?
3. Christians do not discriminate against others because of _____ (mention at least six things).
4. Every person has the right to: _____ (from what we saw in class).
5. No one has the right to force you (using as an excuse that you do not discriminate) to: _____ (mention four things).
6. How does Jesus give us an example of non-discrimination?
7. What did Brainerd answer the old man in the illustration?

Phrases to Memorize

1. No one can dictate how parents in each family educate their children.
2. Christians fight ideas that promote sin, because sin destroys humanity.
3. No one can stop you from expressing your ideas (even if they are against certain groups).
4. No one can stop you (legally, at least in most countries) from openly preaching to them about Jesus
5. Christians do not discriminate against anyone based on their race, nationality, religion, language, where they live, sex, their parents, temperament, economic position, gifts, talents, or abilities, etc.

Other Bible passages on the theme for reading and memorization

2 Tim. 4:1-2; Mt. 7:1-29; 2 Jn. 1:10-11; Jn. 6:37; Col. 3:12-14; Gal. 5:1; Gal. 3:28; Dt. 10:17; 2 Chr. 19:7; Acts. 10:34; Rom. 2:11; Gal. 2:6; Col. 3:25; Jas. 2:9.

70

Use of Social Media

Memorize

Isaiah 41:10 "So do not fear, for I am with you; do not be dismayed, for I am your God. I will strengthen you and help you; I will uphold you with my righteous right hand."

Social media platforms such as FB, YouTube, Instagram, TikTok, WhatsApp, etc. are used by billions of people around the world. Using these platforms is not bad itself, but we have to be wise while using them.

? Introductory Questions

1. Why do you think social media is so popular these days?
2. How do you think social media can affect your daily life?
3. Which social media do you use? How much time per day do you use it?

Bible Story (1 Kings 22:1-37)

Social media is popular because it promises to make people famous. However, there are all kinds of information on it, and much of it is false. For example, a stranger might tell you in a video that something is easy to do, but if you do it, you could put your life at risk. There might also be scantily clad people (which is a very bad thing), and there might be foul language and violence. Social media invites you to have contact with people you don't know, or people you know very little about. Don't have contact with them, only with those that your parents authorize, this is very important. Also, immediately delete those who post bad things.

Many false ideas are preached on social media. Can you name some of them? Non-Christian *influencers* are present, and they lead their followers down a false path. Never follow them. The "like" is addictive, and you may be seeking the approval of men and not of God. Lastly, and most importantly, excessive use of social media wastes valuable time that you need to study and serve the Lord.

In the Bible story, the wicked King Ahab liked to hear only nice words, and he had 400 false prophets to speak to him the words he wanted to hear. But since he had invited King Jehoshaphat (who was a servant of God) to battle, the latter told him that he wanted to consult the Lord through a true prophet. So, they came across Micaiah, who gave them a message from God: a word of judgment. But Ahab, instead of repenting, put God's prophet in jail. What happened in the story was that, as always, God's word was fulfilled, and King Ahab died. This story illustrates the multitude of *influencers* who saturate social media. They speak nicely and prophesize good words, but they are false words, because they are false prophets.

Illustration

An example of the danger of social media is that of Amanda Todd, a teenager from Canada who suffered from cyberbullying. At age 12, Amanda was convinced by a stranger online to send him a photo of an intimate part of her body; but then, the stranger used this image to try to force her to do more. When she refused, the stranger sent the photo to her acquaintances and friends and publicly ridiculed her; then he followed her from time to time, harassing her on social media. Amanda changed schools several times, but the stranger created fake profiles and stalked her to discredit her and cause her to be abandoned by her friends. She felt lonely, took drugs and alcohol, and fell into a deep depression and a lot of anxiety. She felt worthless, and the devil took advantage of all this to advise her to take her life; finally, she did. This true story is a warning to teenagers not to talk to strangers on social media, or consume information that is harmful to their mental health. Why do you think Amanda agreed to talk to this stranger and send him that photo?

Questions About the Class

1. Do you think it is useful to be popular on social media? Yes/No, why?
2. What are the risks of using social media?
3. What should you do when a stranger wants to be your friend?
4. What should you do immediately when someone on your "friends" list posts something inappropriate?
5. Why should you not listen to videos from *influencers* who are not Christians?
6. Do you think you should ask your parents and church teachers about someone who claims to be a Christian who posts videos on YouTube, FB, etc. to find out if it is good or not to listen to them?
7. What does the Bible Story seen in class teach us? What do you think is the main idea of the illustration?

Phrases to Memorize

1. Social media can be an advantage for connecting with other mature Christians.
2. But it can also be addictive and take up valuable time. It can also give you false information.
3. Social media is very dangerous if you have contact with people you don't know. Never talk to strangers, and only talk to people your parents approve of.
4. Use social media sparingly (maybe 15 minutes to half an hour each day, and less is better), and every time you post something, identify yourself as a Christian.
5. Don't share personal information in your posts.

Other Bible passages on the theme for reading and memorization

1 Cor. 15:33; Eph. 4:29; Rom. 1:18-2:8; 1 Jn. 5:19; 1 Ti. 5:13; 2 Cor. 12:20; Prov. 12:16-23; Mt. 7:15; 1 Jn. 4:1; Mt. 24:24; 2 Pet. 2:1; 2 Cor. 11:13-15; Ps. 27:10; Dt. 31:6.

Part VII. Your Identity

71

Your Sex is Your Sex

Memorize

Genesis 1:27 "So God created mankind in his own image, in the image of God he created them; male and female he created them."

God's design for mankind was this: that there would be a man and a woman who would unite in marriage to create a family. If you are a boy, God made you different from girls; and if you are a girl, God made you different from boys. God made you with the sex you have and nothing can change that throughout your life. However, there are some who, due to the deception of the devil, have tried to change their sex, and this is a thought of rebellion before God, and a sin that brings very serious consequences. The devil is a liar, and although his reasons may have some "logic" for sinners, a healthy thought will always say that God's design is the best and the right thing, the rest is sick and wrong.

❓ Introductory Questions

1. What are the differences between boys and girls?
2. What are the things that you do that a boy or a girl do? Did you know that boys' bones are different from girls'?
3. How do your parents help you (if you are a boy) behave like a boy or if you are a girl, behave like a girl?

Bible Story (Genesis 19:1-13)

The Bible tells us a very tragic story in Genesis chapter 19. It was about two cities, Sodom and Gomorrah, which had very sinful people. They were such evil people that they had gone against God's design for the family, which is this: one man must marry one woman. Nevertheless, in those cities, boys wanted to be girls, and girls wanted to be boys, and men married with men and women with women. This way of thinking and actions displeased God so much that He decided to destroy these cities.

The case of the destruction of these two cities is unique in the Bible, and it means that, although there are no small or great sins before God, there are sins that cause more harm than others and destroy humanity more than others. The sin that the inhabitants of Sodom and Gomorrah committed was one of those that are very destructive. Actually, the inhabitants of these cities eventually will destroy themselves.

Illustration

Dad, mom, son and daughter were on their way to a park to spend some time together, but as they were going, suddenly, the traffic stopped: it was a parade of men holding hands with other men and women holding hands with other women. They were waving rainbow flags and shouting. The family could also see some men kissing other men and some women kissing other women. Suddenly the youngest child asked: What is that, Dad? Why are they doing that?

The father, who was a Christian, replied: "This is a parade of men who want to be women and women who want to be men, my son. They have decided to rebel against God and do things that are against their nature. For example, you are a boy and God wanted you to be a boy, and your little sister is a girl and God created her a girl. Both you and your little sister will always be the sex you were created to be. By the way, the rainbow was created by God as a symbol that He always does what He says.

You must be careful of a person who wants to be alone with you; or who wants you to touch hi/her; or who talks to you about sex. You must say <u>no</u> immediately, get away from him or her to a safe place, and tell your parents, as soon as that happens.

Questions About the Class

1. What was God's design for marriage?
2. Why did God destroy Sodom and Gomorrah?
3. Why is it a sin before God to want to have a gender that is not yours?
4. Do people who commit this sin go to heaven? Yes/No, why?
5. What did the illustration's father answer his son when he asked him about the parade? For what purpose did God create the rainbow?
6. What should you do when someone wants to be alone with you? What should you do if someone wants you to touch them or talks to you about sex?

Phrases to Memorize

1. God created marriage, and God's plan will always be this: a man and a woman should marry; and their union is for life and only between the two of them.
2. The devil deceives some and makes them think that God made a mistake in creating them with a man's body or a woman's body; but that is false.
3. Those who rebel against God in this bring a very destructive sin to humanity, that is why God gets so angry with these people.
4. If someone wants you to be alone with him/her, or wants you to touch him/her, or talks to you about sex, you must say <u>no</u> immediately, go to a safe place, and tell your parents immediately, on that same day.

Other Bible passages on the theme for reading and memorization

Lev. 18:22; Rom. 1:32; 1 K. 15:12; Rom. 1:27; Lev. 20:13; 1 Cor. 6:9-11; 1 Ti. 1:8-11; Jdg. 19:16-24; Jud. 1:7; Gn. 19:1-13

72

Beware of Manipulators

Memorize

2 Corinthians 11:14 "And no wonder, for even Satan disguises himself as an angel of light."

You must learn that in this world there are many who manipulate others. This means that these people want others to do what they say without caring about your well-being. They are thinking of taking advantage of the goodwill of others, and many times they want to take us where God does not want us to go. These people may seem good at first, but then they will start telling you to do things that are against what God says. Be careful with them!

? Introductory Questions

1. Have you ever done something bad to get what you want? Yes/no, how do you get what you want?
2. Has another boy or girl ever invited you to places you shouldn't go or to do something you shouldn't do? Tell us about it.
3. Do you know someone who is bossy and controlling at your school? Why do you think these people are not good?

Bible Story (1 Kings 13:1-32)

In 1 Kings chapter 13 we find the story of a prophet of God who was sent to give a word to King Jeroboam. God had told him to give the word to the king and then to return by a different route than he had come, and not to eat with anyone or drink water from anyone.

But on the way, he met an old prophet who invited him to eat. At first the young prophet told him that he would not go with him because God had ordered him not to. But the old prophet manipulated him, tricked him into telling him that an angel of God had spoken to him, telling him to take the prophet who spoke against the Jeroboam's family. So, the young prophet went with him and they ate together. But that was contrary to God's command! And you know what happened? Yes, that's right, you read that right! That prophet died. When he left the old prophet's house, a lion met him on the road and killed him.

This story teaches us that we cannot let ourselves be manipulated by others, because these people will make us stray from God and that can bring us serious consequences.

Illustration

Another good example of manipulation is found in the Word of God. It is the case of Samson. Samson allowed himself to be deceived by women, and those women were evil. Women who had no fear of God and were not Christians. When you read the story of Samson in Judges chapters 13 to 16, you will realize that, although Samson was a very strong man and was a person chosen by God to do great things, the evil women he wanted to be with manipulated him, led him away from God, and finally to death.

You must always remember that your relationship with God comes first and that you must not give in to the proposals of manipulators. They may tell you —like the old prophet— that God told them, or that what they do is a good thing, but you must say <u>no</u> and stay away from such people.

A man and a woman were in a major car accident in which both cars were completely destroyed. However, neither of them were hurt. When they both crawled out of the cars, the woman said to the man, "Look what has happened! You are a man and I am a woman. This is surely a sign from God, who wants us to be united for life." The man saw that the woman was beautiful, and said, "Yes, I do." The woman then continued and said, "Look! The bottle of wine that was in the car has not broken. This is a miracle! It is another sign! Let us drink it now to celebrate our future union and our future weddings." The woman opened it and gave the bottle to the man, who drank half of it. He then gave the bottle to the woman. But the woman did not drink a single drop, but put the cork back in, handed it back to the man and said: "Very well, my friend, now all we have to do is wait for the police to arrive."

❓ Questions About the Class

1. Tell me some characteristics of manipulators
2. In which chapter of 1 Kings is the story of the prophet of God who was sent to King Jeroboam and who was deceived by an old prophet?
3. How did the old prophet deceive the prophet of God?
4. What happened to the prophet of God for having disobeyed God?
5. What does this story teach us?
6. Why is the story of Samson a good example of manipulation?

Phrases to Memorize

1. Manipulators are people who lie or deceive you to get you to do what they want and thus take your time, money, strength, etc.
2. Manipulators are instruments of satan to make you stray from Jesus.
3. The Bible warns us not to let these people manipulate us, and not to be manipulators of others.
4. A Christian is one who convinces others to follow Jesus and do good, and always does everything with honesty and truth.

Other Bible passages on the theme for reading and memorization

Mt.7:15; 2 Ti. 3:1-5; 2 Cor. 11:14; Mt. 24:4; 1 Cor. 13:4-7; Gal. 5:19-21; 1 Ti. 4:1; Gal. 5:1; Rom. 16:18; 2 Ti. 3:6; Eph. 4:25; Mt. 10:16.

73

Suffering is Normal

Memorize

John 16:33 "I have told you these things, so that in me you may have peace. In this world you will have trouble. But take heart! I have overcome the world!"

There are many people in this world who suffer, and you will not be the exception. You may think that you will be the only person in the world who will escape suffering, but that is not true. Suffering will come into your life, one way or another. But two things are very important: 1. The reasons why you suffer; and 2. The decisions you make when you are suffering.

The greatest example we have is in Christ himself. He said that both He and His disciples were going to suffer; and if you want to be a disciple of Jesus, you also have to suffer. However, if you obey the Word of God, not only will you suffer less than those who do not obey it, but everything you suffer in Christ will be for good.

Introductory Questions

1. Do you have any kind of suffering? Which one?
2. Why do you think people suffer in the world?
3. What are some examples of bad decisions that people make and that is why they suffer?

Bible Story (Jeremiah 38:1-13)

Most people suffer because they do wrong, and sin brings suffering. But you should aim to suffer for only two things: because you do good and obey the Lord; and because you preach the word of God (see Matthew 5:10-11). Only for these two things. Then, when you suffer, you should think that God will bring good things into your life. You should, therefore, pray, thanking God and trusting that He will help you. If you suffer for the reasons Jesus gives in Matthew 5:10-11, you should be glad about it.

Jeremiah was a great prophet of God. He obeyed the Lord and spoke what the Lord told him to speak. When he told the people that Judah was going to be defeated by the Babylonians —because the Lord told him to tell them so— his enemies put him in a very deep cistern. At the bottom of the cistern there was mud, and Jeremiah had to be in that dark, muddy place. But God did not abandon him. Do you know what God did? God used a foreigner, an Ethiopian, to free the prophet. He spoke to the king and convinced him to take the prophet out of that pit so that he would not die. Thus, they took the prophet Jeremiah out. This story teaches us that when we obey the Lord, sometimes we will suffer, but God will free us, and take us out of the pit, no matter how deep it is.

Illustration

Our Daily Bread devotional published the story of the orange farmer Parnell Bailey. There had been a severe drought in those days, and on top of that, the irrigation system was broken. The trees in the area where Parnell's orchard was located were in very bad shape, and many were already drying out. However, in Parnell's orchard, the trees were intact; what was the secret? He put it this way: "My trees could go without rain for at least another two weeks. You see, when they were young, I gave them very little water, and sometimes I denied them water altogether. So, these trees developed deeper and deeper roots, seeking moisture. Now my trees are the deepest-rooted in the region. While others are now burning up in the sun, these trees find moisture deeper."

This story teaches us that suffering makes us stronger and prepares us to withstand the great storms in life. Psalms 125:1 says: "Those who trust in the Lord are like Mount Zion, Which cannot be moved but abides forever."

Questions About the Class

1. What are two things that are important about suffering?
2. Who is the greatest example of suffering?
3. What is the difference between those who suffer for disobeying God and those who suffer for obeying Him?
4. What are the two things that Jesus says Christians should be willing to suffer for?
5. Why did Jeremiah suffer? What did his enemies do to him?
6. What does the illustration teach us?

Phrases to Memorize

1. Suffering will come into your life one way or another, but the important thing is *why* you suffer and *how* you respond to suffering.
2. The greatest example of suffering is in Christ and He said that His disciples would also suffer.
3. People who do not follow Christ suffer because of sin. You must be willing to suffer for obeying Jesus and preaching the gospel.
4. When we suffer, we must trust that God will help us, and be patient. We must also be joyful when we suffer for Jesus' sake.
5. If you make the right decisions, suffering will make you stronger and you will be prepared for the great storms of life.

Other Bible passages on the theme for reading and memorization

2 Cor. 12:9-10; Rom. 5:3-5; Ps. 73:26; Prov. 24:16; 1 Jn. 1:9; Phil. 4:4-7; Prov. 28:13; Gal. 6:7; 1 Pet. 5:10; Rom. 8:18; Rom. 8:28; Jas. 1:2-4; Jn. 16:33; Ps. 34:19; Rev. 21:4; 2 Ti. 3:12; Phil. 1:29; 2 Cor. 4:17.

14

Be Generous

Memorize

Proverbs 11:25 "The generous will prosper; those who refresh others will themselves be refreshed."

Generosity is not just about money. You can give work, time, and kind words to others. If you are a generous person with others, God will prosper you; in the Word of God, we have many references regarding this. You do not need to be rich to be generous; just give what you have. Be hospitable and seek to help others as much as you can. When God blesses you with money, seek to give as much as you can without interest in receiving anything in return. The Bible teaches us to give for the support of God's servants and to the poor and needy of the earth.

❓ Introductory Questions

1. How are you being generous?
2. Give me some ideas you that have to be a generous person.
3. What were the examples of generosity of the Lord Jesus?

Bible Story (2 Kings 4:8-37)

The Bible tells us the story of a woman whom God calls *important*. She had resources, and she enjoyed sharing them with the right people. God's word teaches us to share our resources with God's servants. This woman noticed that the prophet Elisha was passing through the city where she and her husband lived (Sunem), so she invited him to eat. But because she wanted to give more, she spoke to her husband and asked him to build a place for God's servant to spend the night. This act of generosity caused God's servant to pray for her, for a need she had had for many years: she and her husband longed for a child. And do you know what happened? God gave them the child that she and her husband longed for.

Later, God tested this woman because the son that God had given them died. However, she went to God's servant and Elisha prayed for him and God resurrected him. This story shows us what the Word says: that the generous soul will be prospered. Always try to be a generous and God will prosper you. Generosity is a sign that we have the spirit of Christ, because Christ gave us that example.

This story also teaches us that a generous person understands and meets the needs of others before they tell them.

Illustration

Timothy Keller told the following story in his book *The Prodigal God: Recovering the Heart of the Christian Faith*. A farmer came to his king to give him a gift. He brought the largest carrot he had ever grown that year. The king, touched by this act of generosity, gave him a piece of land to plant more. One of the nobles

SPIRITUAL RESILIENCE

of the kingdom heard about what the king had done to the poor farmer and went and gave the king a horse, thinking that the king would do the same thing he had done to the poor farmer. However, the king barely thanked him. The nobleman, confused by this, asked the king why he had treated the farmer differently. The king replied: "The poor farmer brought me the largest carrot he had ever grown and gave it to me. But you brought me this horse, and you are giving it to yourself. The farmer thought about me, but you are thinking about yourself."

This story teaches us that when we give we should not expect to receive anything; this is true generosity.

❓ Questions About the Class

1. What are some things we can be generous with?
2. What should be our attitude towards giving? Should we give expecting to receive in return?
3. To whom should we give generously?
4. What was the need that the woman of Shunem saw?
5. What else does the story of Elisha and the woman of Shunem teach us?
6. Why did the king in the illustration give land to the farmer and nothing to the nobleman?

Phrases to Memorize

1. You don't have to be rich to be generous.
2. You can be generous not only with your money, but also with your work, your time, and your kind words.
3. The Bible teaches us to be generous with God's servants and with those in need.
4. Generosity is a sign that we have the spirit of Christ, because Christ set that example for us; and following his example makes us have peace and joy.
5. The generous man always manages to see the needs that others have before they tell him. He takes the initiative to help.
6. The generous man does not expect to receive anything in return for what he has given; nor does he claim any right for what he gives. He simply does it and expects the reward from the Lord.

Other Bible passages on the theme for reading and memorization

Acts. 20:35; Lk. 6:38; Prov. 11:24-25; Prov. 19:17; Lk. 21:1-4; Mt. 6:21; 1 Ti. 6:17-19; 2 Cor. 9:6-11; Mt. 10:42; 1 Jn. 3:17; Prov. 22:9; Prov. 21:13; Mt. 6:1-4; Ps. 112:5; Dt. 15:7-8; Lk. 12:33; Heb. 13:16; Acts. 2:45; Prov. 28:27.

75

Be Humble

Memorize

Proverbs 22:4 "True humility and fear of the LORD lead to riches, honor and long life."

One of the most important characteristics of the character of the Lord Jesus Christ is humility. Humility is the opposite of arrogance or pride. A proud person is someone who thinks he or she is greater or superior to others, or that he or she deserves to be in a high place, on the throne of a king or queen. But when we are humble, eventually, God will give us riches, honor, and life. Do you want to have those things? When we humble ourselves, the Lord promises to exalt us.

❓ Introductory Questions

1. What is the first thing you think of when you hear the word king or queen?
2. Do you know anyone in your class who thinks he or she is more important than others and wants others to obey him or her
3. How do you feel about people who think they are more important than others? Do you like them?

Bible Story (Daniel 4:28-37)

In the Book of Daniel we have the story of a king named Nebuchadnezzar. I know, it's a very long name! Can you pronounce it? Well, this king had a very large and powerful kingdom called Babylon.

One day this king went out to see the gardens he had created. They were very beautiful gardens, the most beautiful in all the land. He also saw the greatness of his palace. Then he said in his heart, "Look at all this that you have done! You are very great, O King Nebuchadnezzar. All this was done by your own strength." These were words of pride and God was not pleased with what the king had in his heart, so a voice came from heaven saying, "The kingdom is taken from you; you will be thrown out from among men, and your dwelling will be with the beasts of the field." God made the king go mad and act like a beast, so the people threw him out of the palace, and he walked around in the fields and grew his nails and was like an animal. This is what happened to him because of his pride. God wants all of us to be humble and recognize that all good things come from Him. He also wants us to be humble before people and recognize others as better than us. We should recognize others as better than ourselves. It is wiser to consider others better than ourselves, and to let others speak well of us (see Proverbs 27:2).

Illustration

Samuel I. Prime wrote the biography of Samuel Morse. Samuel Morse was a great painter and inventor. He was the one who invented the telegraph. The telegraph is no longer used, but about 100 years ago it was an important instrument of communication between distant places.

Samuel Morse became very famous, but he was a very humble man. He once said, "The more I think of the greatness of all that has been accomplished, the more I feel small, and the more I see the hand of God in it all. How He is the One who uses the lives of human beings as His instruments...we are all dependent on God first, and then on each other." When we are humble it will help us to be close to God, and when we are close to God we cannot help but be humble (see Isaiah 57:15).

Questions About the Class

1. What is one of the main characteristics of the Lord Jesus Christ?
2. What is the opposite of humility?
3. How do you identify a proud person?
4. What did King Nebuchadnezzar say that God did not like?
5. What happened to King Nebuchadnezzar because of his pride?
6. Why does Samuel I. Prime say that Samuel Morse was humble? How did he know?

Phrases to Memorize

1. Humility is one of the main characteristics of the Lord Jesus Christ and it should also be ours.
2. To the humble, God will give riches, honor, and life, and He will exalt them; all this will be in the time that He wants.
3. The humility that God wants is that which recognizes others as better and more important than ourselves.
4. God wants us to humble ourselves before Him and before others.
5. We should let others speak well of us, and not us of ourselves.

Other Bible passages on the theme for reading and memorization

Prov. 22:4; Prov. 11:2; Col. 3:12; Jas. 4:10; 1 Pet. 5:5; Jas. 4:6; Eph. 4:2; Mic. 6:8; Prov. 18:12; Prov. 15:33; 2 Chr. 7:14; 1 Pet. 5:6; Lk. 14:11; Phil. 2:3; Rom. 12:3; Prov. 3:34; Prov. 29:23; Ps.149:4.

16

Stay Away from Temptation

Memorize

Matthew 26:41 "Watch and pray so that you will not fall into temptation. The Spirit is willing, but the flesh is weak."

Everyone, even the Lord Jesus Christ, has been tempted, but you cannot be so foolish as to enter into a temptation by yourself. There are voluntary temptations (in which you enter into it alone) and involuntary ones. As for involuntary temptations (like Jesus' in Matthew 4), God will not allow you to be tempted beyond what you can bear, so the temptation you have cannot be compared to that of another. The goal of your life should be to stay away from voluntary temptations as much as possible and to be prepared to overcome involuntary ones.

Introductory Questions

1. How do you think you can avoid temptation?
2. What are the things that are most likely to cause you to sin? Do you think people can make you turn away from God?
3. How can people help you avoid falling into temptation?

Bible Story (Genesis 39:7-12)

Joseph is one of the most important characters in Genesis. He was sold by his brothers and ended up in the house of an Egyptian named Potiphar. Potiphar's wife was a wicked woman, for she set her eyes on Joseph; a good woman would never set her eyes on any man but her husband. When you get married, you cannot have eyes for anyone else but your husband or wife. Well, this woman wanted Joseph to sleep with her; do you remember the lesson about fidelity in marriage? But Joseph was a Christian, and he always said <u>no</u> to her.

One day, Potiphar's wife wanted him to sleep with her by force and grabbed him by the clothes, but he left his clothes in the hands of Potiphar's wife and ran away from there. That is what you should do when you are in a dangerous situation, run away. Never expose yourself to temptation, rather, run away. If you do, you will most likely fall into evil, you should run away immediately, get away. That is, places where there are temptations, people or relationships that can lead you to temptations, habits, movies, T.V. shows, etc. Stay away from anything that suggests you do things that are against the Word of God. You should stay away from people and relationships that induce or guide you to do evil.

Illustration

In a survey of Christian readers of *Discipleship Journal* in 1992, it was found that most people had problems with temptations regarding money, pride, laziness, anger, sexual immorality, envy, overeating, and lying. All those who had problems in any of these areas reported that they spent very little time in prayer, they read the Bible very little, and did not like having anyone to whom they were accountable. Therefore, in order for you to overcome temptations you must do exactly the opposite: spend a lot of time in prayer, in the Word of God, and have people who have access to your life and to whom you are accountable for what is in your heart. These people should be, first, your parents. Jesus said to be alert and pray that we would not enter into temptation; also Psalm 119:11 says, "I have hidden your word in my heart that I might not sin against you." You too can pray that God will help you not to fall into temptation (read Matthew 6:13).

Questions About the Class

1. What is a temptation? Can you give an example of a temptation?
2. Is it good to compare your temptation with that of another? Yes/no, why?
3. What was the temptation that Joseph had? How did he overcome it? Why should you stay away from people who want to make you sin?
4. According to the survey of *Discipleship Journal* readers, what are the areas where people had the most problems with temptation? What were the reasons why they fell into these temptations?
5. Why is it so important to give an account to trustworthy people, for example, your parents?
6. What does Psalms 119:11 say?
7. What is the difference between voluntary and involuntary temptations? Give some examples.

Phrases to Memorize

1. A temptation is any situation that wants to make you sin or lose faith in God.
2. You must do everything in your power to stay away from temptations.
3. There are involuntary temptations (like Jesus'), but you, like Him, must be prepared to overcome them.
4. You must flee from people, movies, social media, habits, and anything that puts you in danger of doing wrong before God.
5. To be prepared to overcome temptation, you must spend time daily in the Bible, in prayer, and you must have people to whom you are accountable.

Other Bible passages on the theme for reading and memorization

1 Cor. 10:13; Jas. 4:7; Gal. 5:16; 1 Cor. 6:18-20; Heb. 2:18; Eph. 6:10-18; Jas. 1:14; Jas. 4:17; Lk. 22:40; Heb. 4:15; Ps. 119:11; 1 Pet. 5:8-11; Mt. 6:13; Rom. 12:2; Jas. 1:12; 1 Jn. 5:4; 1 Jn. l 2:1; 1 Cor. 15:33; Mt. 26:41; 2 Ti. 2:22.

11

Taking Important Decisions

Memorize

Psalms 25:12 "Who are those who fear the LORD? He will show them the path they should choose."

Certainly, life is made up of decisions. You are the result of the decisions your parents have made, but soon, you will be the result of the decisions you make now and in the future. No one wants to make bad decisions, but if they don't know how to make good decisions, then they will have a life of failure. Every day, you make small decisions, and those small decisions prepare you for the bigger decisions of your life. You own your decision, but not the *result* of that decision.

❓ Introductory Questions

1. What do you think are the most important decisions you have to make in life?
2. How are you preparing yourself to make those decisions?
3. Do you know people who have made bad decisions in the areas you mentioned in question 1?

Bible Story (1 Kings 12:1-20)

You could say that a big decision is one whose result will bring you much happiness or, on the contrary, much suffering. It will make things easier or more difficult for you, it will make you lose time, or it will make you save time.

An important decision is like embarking on a journey: if you make a mistake in where you are going, you may not have enough time to get back and take the right path. The most important decisions in life are these: 1. Accept Jesus as your Savior and Lord (determines where you will spend eternity); 2. Who you will marry (this decision can bring you great happiness or the opposite); 3. What you will do (this takes up a good part of your time in life).

Rehoboam was the son of King Solomon and was king after his father over all Israel. However, when he began to reign, he wanted to establish his kingdom and asked for advice. First, he spoke to the elders. They told him that he should be less harsh than his father, because his father had been very demanding and asked for too much. Then Rehoboam went to the young men, those who had grown up with him. And they advised him to be harsh, even harsher than his father, and to demand even more from them than Solomon. So, Rehoboam took the advice of the young and told the people His decision. When the people heard Rehoboam's words, they rebelled against him and the kingdom was divided. This decision cost Rehoboam much loss and his kingdom was greatly reduced. What should Rehoboam have done to make a good decision?

Illustration

John Ortberg wrote in his book *All the Places to Go... How Will You Know?*, a study made by a certain research agency. They found that, on average, a person makes seventy decisions every day. This works out to 25,500 decisions per year and almost two million over a lifetime. So, who you are today represents the sum of all those decisions. That's why you have to be very careful about making small decisions, because small decisions prepare you for bigger ones.

Guide to making good decisions every day:

1. Go to God's Word always, every day, to receive the Lord's direction.
2. Go to God in prayer every day so that the Holy Spirit can clarify your thoughts.
3. Use your common sense and good reasoning.
4. Go to wise counsel (your parents, and your pastors).
5. Compare the requirements with the realities, and leave feelings as something secondary.

❓ Questions About the Class

1. What is life made of (according to the lesson)?
2. You are the result of _____.
3. What is it that prepares you to make the biggest decisions in your life?
4. You own your decision and also the result of that decision. True/false. Why true/false?
5. What are the three most important decisions in life?
6. Why did Rehoboam make a bad decision?
7. What is the guide to making good decisions every day?

Phrases to Memorize

1. What you will be the result of your own decisions now and in the future.
2. You must learn to make good decisions (see the guide to making good decisions).
3. You are the owner of your decision, but not of the result of that decision.
4. The three most important decisions: to follow Jesus; who you will marry; and what you will do.
5. Do <u>not</u> rush into making important decisions, follow the decision-making guide and take all the time you need. However, the decision to follow Jesus must be made right now, because delaying doing so will always work against you.

Other Bible passages on the theme for reading and memorization

Prov. 3:5-6; Jas. 1:5; Prov. 11:14; Is. 30:21; Jas. 3:17; Prov. 16:33; Jn. 5:30; Prov. 12:15; Jos. 24.15; Prov. 18:15; Ps. 25:4; Prov. 15:22; Ps. 32:8; Ps. 119:105; Prov. 16:9; Rom. 8:28; Prov. 2:6.

78

Don't Live by Emotions

Memorize

Jeremiah 17:9 "The heart is deceitful above all things, and desperately sick; who can understand it?"

Since the beginning of the world, people have made many bad decisions based on feelings. They say, "I have to listen to what my heart tells me," but they do not know that the mind and heart can be moved by the desires of sin and by satan. We, as Christians, cannot make decisions or live based on feelings, but always on the will of God. We must always ask ourselves, would Jesus do this? What does the Bible say about this? Is it right? Sometimes we may "feel" like doing bad things or "feel" like not doing the things we should, but we must say no to all of these things.

❓ Introductory Questions

1. Have you ever felt like doing things you shouldn't do?
2. Do you sometimes feel like not doing things you should do? What do you decide?
3. Why do you think it is very dangerous to make decisions based on feelings?

Bible Story (Matthew 26:36-46)

On several occasions, Jesus told his disciples that he was going to the cross. He was never afraid of dying or in doubt: He was determined to suffer and die for us because that was God's will. In addition to the torture and horrendous death that any of us might suffer for the sake of Christ, the Lord had to bear the sins of the world. This was a very big thing: He would become the greatest of sinners for our sake; something that distressed him greatly, because there would come a time when he would literally be abandoned by the heavenly Father.

Jesus then went to a garden to pray. In that place, the Lord asked his Father to help him endure this abandonment (Mt. 27:46). Jesus never refused to suffer for us and give his life for the world, because he never made decisions based on feelings, he did what he had to do, and he fulfilled his mission completely. Thus, we must do the will of God in everything and not let ourselves be carried away by what we feel, because this is often deceptive. When we do the will of God we will have joy in the Holy Spirit.

Illustration

One of the most common examples of this is the case of a Christian girl who is courted by an unsaved boy. This boy treats her well, is kind, attentive, shows her a lot of affection. In addition, he is physically attractive, intelligent, and has money. The girl thinks that, although he is not a Christian, she could live happily with this boy if they were married, and she begins to think about it. All of this, of course, is a trap of the devil. You <u>must not allow</u> love stories to develop in your mind (fantasies); that does not come from God.

She thinks that later he, since he is a very good boy, will accept the gospel and become a Christian. She starts inviting him to church, and he accepts; then he pretends to have become a Christian, and is baptized (he does it all for the girl's interest, not because he has been converted). What would you do in that case? She becomes the boy's girlfriend. Her parents are Christians, and they advise her to leave him, telling her that if she marries him later she will have to suffer a lot and be unhappy. She disobeys them, and finally marries him. From the first day, the boy shows that he is not really converted to Christ, and he opposes the gospel. The girl has to suffer unnecessarily, and later she regrets the decision she has made. She let herself be carried away by her emotions; she "listened to her heart," but her heart has deceived her, as Jeremiah 17:9 says.

Questions About the Class

1. People always make good decisions based only on their feelings. True/False, why?
2. What should you base your decisions on?
3. What was Jesus' intention regarding the cross? Did he want to go to the cross or not? Was there ever a time when Jesus hesitated to do God's will?
4. What is the difference between the suffering we can experience for Christ's sake and Christ's suffering?
5. What was the mistake that the Christian girl in the illustration made? Why did she make such a serious mistake?

Phrases to Memorize

1. People make bad decisions based on feelings, don't be one of them.
2. Christians make decisions based on the will of God expressed in the Bible.
3. We must, like Jesus, be determined to do the will of God and not follow emotions.
4. The joy that Christians experience is from the Holy Spirit (Rom. 14:17).
5. If you make decisions based on feelings, you will have to suffer and you will lose very valuable time.

Other Bible passages on the theme for reading and memorization

Phil. 4:6-7; Prov. 29:11; Prov. 15:18; Gal. 5:16-24; Rom. 12:2; Ecc. 3:4; Jos. 1:9; Rom. 12:15; 2 Ti. 1:7; Prov. 15:13; Eph. 4:26-27; Prov. 25:28; Prov. 16:32; Jas. 1:20; Rom. 14:17.

19

The Meaning of "Good Life"

Memorize

Psalms 16:11 "You make known to me the path of life; you will fill me with joy in your presence, with eternal pleasures at your right hand."

You must always go to God's Word to find out what God thinks about life's most important questions. The world has answers, but the world's answers will not always coincide with God's mind; rather, more often than not, they will be in opposition to it. If you base yourself on the world's concept of living the *good life*, you will always live dissatisfied, full of fear, sadness, and feeling like a failure.

? Introductory Questions

> 1. What is the meaning of a *good life* for you?
> 2. What would your classmates at school tell you if you asked them the question above?
> 3. Did Jesus live a good life (read Matthew 8:20)?

Bible Story (Matthew 19:16-21)

Many people followed Jesus because He did much good for others. He healed the sick, freed the demon-possessed, and preached the gospel to them. Jesus taught people the true meaning of life, for He knows all things, and He desires for us to have life, and abundant life.

One day, a young man who had a lot of wealth came to ask Jesus something. This young man, although he had a lot of money to "enjoy life" —according to the world's concept— had a great emptiness inside him. He knew that something was missing, but he did not know exactly what it was. So, he went and asked Jesus, "Good Teacher, what good thing must I do to have eternal life?" Jesus thought about the good thing this young man had: that he recognized that He (Jesus) is God, and that he obeyed the commandments. However, he knew that there was something that was preventing him from entering eternal life: he needed to leave what he thought was "the good life." It was precisely riches —what he thought, and most people think— that is the good life, which prevented him from enjoying the true good life that God gives. This good life is in giving the fruit of the Holy Spirit, and the earthly riches were an obstacle for this young man to be able to produce it. Do you know what the *fruit of the Spirit* is?

Illustration

Have you ever stopped to think about how electricity is produced? You probably know that electricity is not in the outlet where you plug in a computer, for example. You know that electricity comes from somewhere far away. Wires are conductors of electricity, but they do not produce it. When there is electricity in your house, then there is light in your house, right? The light that you have is the result or the fruit of the electric energy that has reached your house, and it is the sign that you have electricity. The fruit of the Spirit is like that light. You have the fruit of the Spirit when the Holy Spirit is turned on in you. The fruit of the Spirit is: *love, joy, peace, patience, kindness* (sweetness, gentleness), *goodness* (giving good things), *faith, meekness* (not getting angry), *self-control*. Just as a wire does not produce electricity, but only conducts it, so you: the one who produces the fruit of the Spirit is the Holy Spirit. The true meaning of living a good life is to manifest that fruit naturally. You don't have to make an effort for it, or do anything, just be connected to Jesus (read John 15:5) so that you have that fruit.

❓ Questions About the Class

1. What does Jesus want based on what we saw in today's lesson?
2. What did the rich young man come to ask Jesus? Why did he ask him that?
3. What was it that this rich young man could not let go of, which was keeping him from having the life of God?
4. What does it really mean to have a good life?
5. What was it that was keeping the rich young man from being able to bear or produce the fruit of the Spirit?
6. Can you explain how electricity serves as an example to explain the fruit of the Spirit?
7. What are the qualities of the Fruit of the Spirit? (one of them is love).
8. What do you need to do to bear the fruit of the Spirit?

Phrases to Memorize

1. When you are with Jesus, you will always manifest the fruit of the Spirit.
2. Bearing this fruit is the true meaning of living a good life.
3. Jesus wants you and I to bear this fruit, that is why He came and approached us. Now He expects us to approach Him and stay close (connected) to Him.
4. The world thinks that the good life consists of having riches and pleasures, but that is false, because created things will never produce what only the Creator can produce: the fruit of the Spirit in you.
5. Just as a cable does not produce electricity but only conducts it, so you cannot produce the fruit of the Spirit on your own, rather, you have to stay united to Jesus.
6. The fruit of the Spirit is: love, joy, peace, patience, kindness (sweetness, gentleness), goodness (that you give good things), faith, meekness (that you do not get angry), temperance (that you have self-control).

Other Bible passages on the theme for reading and memorization

1 Cor. 4:2; 1 Pet. 4:10-11; 1 Ti. 5:8; Ps. 24:1; 1 Cor. 12:4-6; Mt. 25:14-30; 1 Cor. 10:31; Jas. 1:17; Rom. 12:6-8; 1 Ti. 4:14; Exo. 35:10; 2 Ti. 1:6; Mt. 5:14-16.

80

God is Always Good

Memorize

Genesis 1:31 "And God saw every thing that he had made, and, behold, it was very good. And the evening and the morning were the sixth day."

One of the great qualities of God is that He is good. God's goodness is far more than you and I can imagine. It is everywhere! It is in the nature we all enjoy, it is in human beings, it is in science and in the arts; we can see God's goodness wherever we are and it is always around us.

Introductory Questions

1. What are the things you enjoy most in life? What does God have to do with those things?
2. How could God's goodness be in a prison?
3. Look around you. Can you see God's goodness in what's there? Tell us about that goodness.

Bible Story (Exodus 17:1-7)

The Israelites had seen God's goodness very clearly. They witnessed the miracles He performed on their behalf to free them from the land of Egypt, where they were slaves. Then, when they were trapped between the Red Sea and Pharaoh's army, the good Lord parted the Red Sea for them to pass through on dry land. He gave them bread to eat and water; He protected them from the cold and the heat, and He healed them of their diseases.

But one day, just a few days after they had enjoyed all these blessings, they ran out of water, and then they doubted God's goodness, and complained against Moses. They were so angry that they even wanted to stone him. So, Moses cried out to God and He, in His patience and kindness, gave them all water to drink. However, it had been a great sin to have doubted the goodness of God, the same one who had done so much for them. You, as a son or daughter of God, never doubt the goodness of God. No matter what happens, God's goodness will always be present, you just need to open your eyes and see it.

Illustration

Allen Gardiner was a British missionary to South America. After the death of his first wife, Brother Allen entered the mission field in 1834 and did missionary work in Africa until 1838. Then, from 1838 to 1843, missionary Allen worked among the natives of Chile and traveled to Tierra del Fuego (at the southern tip of the American continent). After making trips to South America and suffering various hardships, in 1851, when Allen Gardiner was 57 years old, he decided to go with others to an island called Picton. But on that island the people were hostile, and the climate very cold. After some time, brother Allen and his companions had to face the terrible situation that their supplies had run out, and it seemed that new food would never get them. Without food, each member of the group was dying of hunger, one by one. Meanwhile, Brother Allen wrote in his journal what was happening each day, and the last thing he wrote, his last line before he died, and in a shaky hand (because of his great weakness), was this: "I am amazed to understand the immense goodness of God." Missionary Allen is believed to have died on September 6, 1851.

God's goodness has been especially manifested by sending His Son Jesus to die for us. When you become a son or daughter of God, the blessings you have are not only those enjoyed by those who do not know God, but He gives you the privilege of His presence, and He gives you eternal life. God's goodness toward His children is special because you have the company of Jesus and His Holy Spirit, and He makes you like Him. Becoming like Jesus is the greatest of God's goodness and grace!

❓ Questions About the Class

1. What were some of the demonstrations of God's kindness toward the Israelites?
2. What made the Israelites doubt God's kindness? Is this good? Yes/No, why?
3. What do you need to do to see God's kindness?
4. Who was Allen Gardiner?
5. What did brother Allen Gardiner write in his journal before he died?
6. How is God's kindness especially manifested in his children?
7. What is the greatest thing about God's kindness toward human beings?

Phrases to Memorize

1. We can see God's goodness in the physical world, in the human body, in the goodness of people (even those who are not Christian), in science and technology, in the arts, etc. God's goodness is free for everyone.
2. Doubting God's goodness is a great sin, and you must be careful never to commit it.
3. You must ask the Lord to open your eyes to see His goodness in the moments when the devil lies to you and prevents you from seeing it.
4. The greatest demonstration of God's goodness is that He sent His Son to save us.
5. If you have the company of Jesus and the Holy Spirit, you will enjoy the greatest of God's goodness and grace, and He will make you like Him.

Other Bible passages on the theme for reading and memorization

1 Cor. 4:2; 1 Pet. 4:10-11; 1 Ti. 5:8; Ps. 24:1; 1 Cor. 12:4-6; Mt. 25:14-30; 1 Cor. 10:31; Jas. 1:17; Rom. 12:6-8; 1 Ti. 4:14; Exo. 35:10; 2 Ti. 1:6; Mt. 5:14-16.

81

Control Your Feelings

Memorize

Proverbs 12:16 "The vexation of a fool is known at once, but the prudent ignores an insult."

Vexation: offense; a cause of trouble.

Emotions were created by God for your good, and to serve Jesus; however, they can also be used by the enemy to harm you and lead you to sin. Therefore, you must control them and be your master, and not let them control you; because if this happens, the devil will use them to harm you and harm others. In order for you to control your emotions, you must place them at the feet of Jesus Christ.

Introductory Questions

1. Name the emotions that you know. Can you define some of them?
2. Are there good emotions and bad ones? Yes/no, why?
3. How can your emotions lead you to do wrong? Give at least one example, two if possible.

Bible Story (Genesis 4:7-11)

Emotions are not good or bad in and of themselves, but will turn into something good or something bad depending on the reason. For example, being sad is not a bad thing in and of itself, and you should even be sad when others are suffering (see Rom. 12:15). But if you are sad because you are selfishly desiring something and not getting something you want or because you are doubting God's goodness, then that feeling reflects sin. The same will be true of all other emotions. However, there are emotions that are more closely related to sin than others (see Eph. 4:31 and Col. 3:8).

In Genesis 4 we have the case of the first two brothers, Cain and Abel. The Bible says that both Cain and Abel each presented their offering before God; however, Abel's offering was accepted by Him, while Cain's was not. The reason why Cain's offering was not accepted was not because of the offering itself, that is, it was not because Cain's offering was of less value than Abel's; rather, God saw the hearts of each one, and He knew that there was no sincerity in Cain's heart. Thus, Cain became angry with his brother and walked around with his head downcast. Which situation would justify Cain feelings? (See Ex. 32:19; Neh. 2:1-4). Cain ended up killing his brother. The same thing happened with Ahaz and Naboth, his neighbor, when Ahaz killed him because Naboth did not want to sell him his land (read 1 Kings 21:1-15) do you remember that story?

Illustration

In his book *The Jubilee Story of the China Inland Mission,* Marshall Broomhall wrote about the life of Mary Dyer. She was born in 1837 in the mission field of China, where her parents were the first missionaries. When her parents died, when she was still very young, she was raised by an uncle. However, the loss of her parents did not stop young Mary, who had a great heart to preach the gospel. Therefore, at the age of 16, she returned alone to China to work as a missionary in a girls' school. Five years later, Mary married Hudson Taylor, one of the most well-known missionaries to this day for his ministry of faith and sacrifice.

Mary's case is a case of mastering her emotions. She obeyed the voice of God who commanded her (as He commands us all): "You shall love the Lord your God with all your heart..." (Loving the Lord is an order!). Mary did not let the feelings of the loss of her parents control her to abandon the mission to China. Jesus wants us to obey Him and walk with Him, and to love Him before anything or anyone. God commands us to govern our emotions: we must love what God loves and hate what God hates; and let the Holy Spirit control our emotions. If the Holy Spirit gives us the power, then we can govern our emotions by His power.

Questions About the Class

1. Why did God create your emotions?
2. How can you be the one who controls your emotions?
3. Are there good emotions and bad ones? Yes/No, why?
4. When is it good to be sad? Now, when is it a reflection of sin?
5. In what cases mentioned in the Bible Story was anger motivated by sin?
6. Why was Mary Dyer's case that of a woman whose emotions were at the feet of Jesus?
7. Is placing our emotions at the feet of Christ optional? Yes/No, why? How can we do this?

Phrases to Memorize

1. Your emotions were created for you to serve the Lord, not yourself.
2. If you don't control your emotions, they will control you to do what displeases God.
3. Emotions are not good or bad in themselves, but the motives why you have them is what is good or bad.
4. There are emotions that are more related to sin than others, for example, sadness, anger, and fear (which, many times, are not for the right reasons).

Other Bible passages on the theme for reading and memorization

Prov. 16:32; 2 Pet. 1:5-9; Eph. 6:11-17; Eph. 4:26-27; Eph. 4:26-27,31; Col. 3:8; Prov. 12.16; Prov. 25:28; 1 Jn. 2:16; Lk. 6:45; Jos. 1:9; Prov. 29:11.

82

Be a True Man

Memorize (only boys)

1 Kings 2:2 "I am about to go the way of all the earth. Be strong, and show yourself a man."

The definition of being a real man in our generation is very different from the definition of God, the Creator of masculinity and femininity. If you walk through life with the wrong idea, you will make serious mistakes and offend even the people you love the most and who love you the most. The correct definition of a *true man* is God's, not the people of the world. This is what I will be talking about in this lesson.

❓ Introductory Questions

1. What is your own definition of being a *true man*?
2. What are the differences that you find between a man and a woman besides the physical differences?
3. What is the definition that your classmates at school have of what a real man should be?

Explanation of Concepts

The definition of a true man is found in Jesus. Jesus is the perfect man and the model of what a true man is. What are the characteristics of Jesus? What is Jesus like as described in the Bible, the Word of God? A true man...

1. He puts Jesus Christ before anyone else on earth, even before his family. Jesus is before everything and before everyone (see Luke 14:26). So too, Jesus put his obedience to Heavenly Father first.
2. He is not afraid to be alone. If others abandon him because he obeys God, he is not afraid. Jesus said to his apostles, when many were abandoning him, "Will you also go away?" (John 6:66-69). Jesus did not start crying and say, "Please do not abandon me! I will do whatever you want." God has said, "I will never leave you nor forsake you" (Heb. 13:5).
3. He is disciplined to seek God in prayer and in the Bible (see Mark 1:35).
4. He always tells the truth, even when the truth seems to be against him; and he is not afraid to denounce injustice and sin (Matt. 23).
5. He is responsible to his family. Jesus fulfilled his responsibilities as a man even while hanging on the cross (John 19:26). A true man never abandons his family and is always there to feed, protect and lead them; he is a true leader of his home.
6. He lives in holiness while single, but if he gets married, he treats his wife with love and gentleness and disciplines his children firmly (but with love).
7. Like Jesus, a true man loves everyone, but does not compromise his faith. He is not rude or proud, but is sincere and humble in heart.
8. Jesus went through great sufferings, and endured terrible pain, but he never complained, nor did he feel sorry for himself saying "poor me," nor did he blame others.

SPIRITUAL RESILIENCE

9. He acquires knowledge, seeks to be taught by others, and knows how to be under authority. Jesus said, "I have come in my Father's name" (John 5:43).
10. He keeps his word and is faithful to the promises he makes before God and others.
11. He always depends on the Holy Spirit to make his own decisions and meditates before making a commitment.
12. He works hard and moves forward with determination until he finishes what he has started. He is honest and responsible in his work. (Luke 9:51).
13. The real man looks like a man. Jesus had his muscles worked out in the carpentry shop, and he most likely did not have long hair. Jesus looked like a man in every way.
14. The real man is formed during childhood, but, since he is obedient to his parents, he is a beloved son, like Jesus (Mt. 3:17).
15. He always behaves kind, gentle, and respectful toward everyone. Then, as a husband, he is faithful, respectful, and loving toward his wife.

❓ Questions About the Class

1. What if your father or mother did not want you to be a Christian? Should you stop being a Christian to obey them? Yes/No, why?
2. Which of the concepts mentioned above are related to being a courageous person? Why is it so important for a man to be courageous?
3. Which of the characteristics mentioned of a true man should a true woman also have? Which of them should not?
4. Give examples of love and respect that a married man should show to his wife.
5. What would you do if your classmates at school discriminated against you for being a Christian?

Phrases to Memorize

1. Love Jesus before everything and everyone.
2. Fear no one but God; but obey the authorities God has given.
3. Be disciplined to pray and seek Jesus in the Bible.
4. Be an obedient and beloved son; but prepare to be a leader of your family.
5. Live in holiness as a single man and then, when you get married, too.
6. Stay humble, don't be proud.
7. Don't complain, feel sorry for yourself, or blame others for your actions.
8. Keep your word and be faithful to the promises you make.
9. Work hard at your work and don't leave it until it's finished.
10. Always depend on the Holy Spirit for everything in life.
11. Look and behave physically like a man in every way.

Other Bible passages on the theme for reading and memorization

1 Cor. 16:13-14; 1 Pet 3:7; 1 Cor. 13:11; 1 K. 2:2-4; Eph. 5:25, 28; Gn. 1:27; 1 Ti. 5:8; Jn. 15:13; Gal. 5:22-23; Ps. 1:1-6; Col. 3:19; Prov. 27:17; Lam. 3:27; 1 Cor. 10:13; Gn. 2:15; Heb. 12:7.

83

Be a True Woman

Memorize (ladies only)

Proverbs 31:30 "Charm is deceitful, and beauty is vain, but a woman who fears the LORD is to be praised."

Although today's woman, compared to that of the last century, for example, has changed greatly, her original design is the same. God has designed woman to be loved and protected, but in order to receive these benefits, she needs to behave like a true woman according to God's design. Certainly, neither man is greater than woman nor woman greater than man, but if they follow God's design for each other, they will complement each other and live happily.

? Introductory Questions

1. What do you think is the biggest difference between a man and a woman besides their physical body?
2. What does it mean to you to be a great woman?
3. How is the great woman you described in the previous question similar to and different from Mary, the mother of Jesus?

Explanation of Concepts

God made man first, and from man, God took the material to make woman. Therefore, woman comes from man in her original design (1 Cor. 11:8), and this as a sign for man to exercise authority over his wife with love and honor, just as Jesus did with His church (Eph. 5:24). However, men born from Eve were taken from her body, this as a sign from God of a mutual need between man and woman, and of the authority of the mother over her children. Likewise, God did not want man to have a perfect companion but woman (for she is his helper), and she cannot feel truly safe and loved without the leadership of man. However, for God, both are equal. Now we will look in more detail at the characteristics of God's design for woman. A true woman...

1. She establishes the family. A woman was made to establish the family, the fundamental foundation of society and of the Church of Christ. She finds her world in the close relationships she has with her family, her husband and her children (Prov. 14:1).
2. She strengthens the man. A woman strengthens her husband's emotions and leadership in the home, because she knows that if the leader is strong, the entire family is strong (see Prov. 31:11-12).
3. She receives —because of her work and her correct attitudes— praise from her husband and her children (Prov. 31:28-29).
4. If she does not have a husband or children, or is left alone, she dedicates herself to serving Christ (1 Tim. 5:5; Luke 2:36-37).
5. She nourishes and grows. A woman is made to nourish and grow. When you were in your mother's womb, she fed you from her body; then, when you were a baby, she continued to feed you (with her

breasts) and will do so as long as she is able. Women who, for whatever reason, do not marry or who cannot have babies do not cease to have that nature, and a real woman will participate in this in one way or another (with adopted children, for example).

6. The true woman is delicate. The apostle Peter calls her "a weaker vessel" (1 Pet. 3:7). She was created to be protected by man in all aspects of life. If a woman has been mistreated because of that fragility, she, <u>deceived by the devil</u>, will cease to be a true woman, that is, she will want to be as strong as the man who took advantage of her delicacy. This is a problem that many women have today, but Christ frees women to be as feminine as the one God created at the beginning.

7. The true woman is capable of growing in intimacy, but she reserves the highest degrees of intimacy for her husband. Intimacy is a process that finds its final stages in marriage, with her husband. He is the one who shares the last stage of her intimacy, that is, her physical body. And in all this process she manifests vulnerability.

   [Note 1]: The word vulnerability is the quality of vulnerable. This means that she could be hurt both physically and morally or emotionally. The true woman is like this because she is designed to be protected by the man. And the true man will always protect the woman. A very important function of the father is to protect his wife and children (it is natural for a real man to be a protector). What about those who do not have a man to protect them? [(ask your teacher)].

   [Note 2]: In the next class, we will see more about the subject of intimacy.

8. A true woman has the desire to be <u>beautiful</u>. The beauty she desires is first internal, which only the Holy Spirit can give, but she is also concerned with external beauty, that is part of her nature as a woman; that is how God designed her. A woman must look like a woman and there is a huge physical difference between a woman and a man, but the beauty that a true woman seeks first is internal, which only God can give.

   [Note]: 1 Pet. 3.3-5 tells us about the true beauty of a woman. Proverbs 31:30 also says: "Charm is deceitful, and beauty is vain; a woman who fears the Lord, she shall be praised."

❓ Questions About the Class

1. Is God's design for woman the same as for man, and are their roles identical? Yes/No, why?
2. How will man and woman become happy with their nature?
3. What is the sign of a man's authority over a woman?
4. What is the sign of a woman's authority over her children? What is the sign of a man's dependence on a woman?
5. What is a man's perfect companion (helpmate)?
6. What is a woman's role in the family?
7. How does a woman strengthen and build up her family?
8. What should a woman do when she is alone?
9. What does it mean that a true woman is delicate? What does it mean that she wants to be beautiful?
10. For whom does a true woman reserve the last stages of intimacy?
11. Explain a woman's desire to be beautiful.

Phrases to Memorize

1. For a woman to have peace, security, and happiness, she must follow God's design for her.
2. God's design for women is very different from that of men.
3. Men and women complement each other, and neither is greater than the other; they make a team.
4. The Christian woman recognizes and respects the authority of the man in the family to make her home strong.
5. The woman makes her family strong when she makes her husband strong as the leader of the family and cooperates with him.
6. The woman who strengthens her family is praised by her husband and her children, and finds happiness.
7. The woman was designed to nurture.
8. The woman is delicate, but she is a leader in the matter of intimacy in relationships.
9. The woman has by nature the desire to be beautiful, but the woman of God is concerned first with internal beauty (which is the best and most important).
10. Woman is as intelligent and as capable as man, but she uses her abilities within the framework of God's design for her.

Other Bible passages on the theme for reading and memorization

Is. 49:15-16; Ps. 131:2; Is. 66:13; 1 Ts. 2:7; Tit. 2:3-5; Prov. 14:1; Prov. 31:10-31; Prov. 11:22; Prov. 18:22; Prov. 19:14; 1 Pet. 3:5; Eph. 5:22-24; 1 Cor. 11:12; 1 Cor. 11:3; 1 Ti. 2.9-12; Gal. 3:28; Ps. 113.9; 1 Pet. 3:7; Lk. 2:36-38.

84

Levels of Intimacy

Memorize

Proverbs 4:23 "Above all else, guard your heart, for everything you do flows from it."

In this class, we will see a topic that you must be very careful to put into practice. The topic of relationships between human beings is very important, and you must be wise and choose very well with whom you share your life. Sharing life has to do with different degrees of intimacy. Intimacy means going deeper, knowing someone's heart more deeply. In the case of those who like each other (a Christian boy and girl), emotional intimacy must come first before physical contact, and the latter can <u>only</u> be in the realm of marriage.

You must minimize any physical contact with anyone else (other than your husband or wife) during your life to only the bare minimum. If you scale the levels of intimacy correctly, then you will have joy and peace in your relationships. You must learn that you should not kiss anyone other than your husband or wife. Kissing before marriage is a sign of distorted levels of intimacy.

❓ Introductory Questions

1. How do you see the behavior of boys who have already had sexual intimacy?
2. What does the word *intimacy* mean to you?
3. Why do you think it is so common to see two people kissing on the mouth? Do you think that if it is common, it is okay? Yes/no, why?

Levels of intimacy

1. <u>Level one</u>: safe communication. Data, information. At this level, feelings, opinions, or personal information that could make you vulnerable are not transmitted.
2. <u>Level two</u>: the opinions and beliefs of others. At this level, we repeat what others have said without saying exactly what we think or believe. When we make these types of statements, we can see the other person's reaction, without making what we have said our own.
3. <u>Level three</u>: my personal opinion and beliefs. At this level, we begin to open up and the level of vulnerability begins, as we start to say what we personally believe and think about something.
4. <u>Level four</u>: my feelings and experiences. At this level, vulnerability grows, as we share our joys, what has caused us pain, our mistakes, our dreams, and our goals. Also, what we like and dislike. We become more vulnerable because we cannot change our past, nor can we change (at least immediately) our tastes. At this level, we risk being criticized and rejected, although we can say that we are not what we were, and this statement is probably convincing.
5. <u>Level five</u>: My needs, emotions, and desires. This is the highest level of intimacy, the deepest part of who we really are. Talking at this level requires a high level of trust; therefore, we need to be absolutely sure that we will not be rejected. If I communicate who I really am, there is no way to convince the

person of anything different. Examples: "I like it when you...", "I need you to do... (such a thing) to feel...", "I want to be with you... because you make me feel..."
6. <u>Level Six</u>: Sexual Intimacy. This level has been designed by God to be enjoyed only in marriage between a woman and a man. This level can be fully enjoyed only after you have previously gone through the lower levels of intimacy, and, of course, after you have already got married.

Climbing the levels of intimacy

1. <u>Managing the levels</u>. It is very important to properly manage the levels of intimacy. As we saw in the class on friends, you must be selective with whom you wish to have dealings and with whom you will have a deeper friendship. In the case of a Christian young man and a Christian young woman who like each other, they must be sure that it is God's will and move forward in the levels of intimacy slowly. The woman is the one who must be the leader here, that is, she is the one who advances first in the levels of intimacy, but she must wait for the man to move after her, otherwise she must not continue.
2. <u>Advancing in the levels of intimacy takes time</u>. You should not rush to advance in the levels of intimacy, be patient. Wait for God to direct things. While this is happening, you should pray and keep your parents informed, and ask them for advice. You should always pray for your relationships, and the person who will marry you should first be a friend that you have known very well; a good Christian with whom you have reached level five of intimacy. Remember to guard your heart, this means that you should always be prepared to run away from a relationship that God does not want. For example, a sign that you should run away will be if the young man (it will almost always be the young man who makes the initiative) wants to touch you or kiss you.
3. <u>When you reach level five</u>. The last level of intimacy can only be with people you trust a lot, like your parents and your siblings. But then you could extend it with the person who will be your husband or wife. Remember, even if you reach this level, it does not mean that you cannot run away if God tells you to, you must always guard your heart, because your heart is a source of life, that is your means of protection. When you have reached that level with someone who is a candidate to be your husband or wife, then you will be ready to get married. Remember to include your parents in the whole process, from the beginning.

<u>Note</u>: I recommend not starting a process leading to marriage before the age of 20.

❓ Questions About the Class

1. What does intimacy mean?
2. What does this lesson recommend regarding kissing?
3. What can you say about physical contact in general according to the class?
4. What happens if you scale correctly in the levels of intimacy?
5. What is level one?
6. What is level two?
7. Can you explain level three?
8. What are levels four and five?

> 9. In the case of a Christian young man and Christian young woman who like each other, who should advance in the levels? What should the Christian young man do to make her advance?
> 10. Two things you should always do when moving forward in a relationship (whether it's friendship or moving towards marriage).
> 11. What are the prerequisites for allowing a Christian young man or Christian young woman to advance in your levels of intimacy?
> 12. What does it mean to "guard your heart"?
> 13. Can you give an example of when you should run away from a relationship?

Phrases to Memorize

1. You must be very careful with whom you spend your time.
2. Sharing life has to do with different degrees or levels of intimacy.
3. Physical contact should be reserved for marriage, that includes kissing.
4. You must correctly scale the levels of intimacy to have joy and peace in your relationships.
5. Level one is information; level two is the opinions and beliefs of others; level three is personal opinions and beliefs; level four is feelings and experiences; and level five is needs, emotions, and desires (everything you really are).
6. You should always pray and ask your parents for advice regarding all your relationships, both friends and someone you like.
7. Progress in the levels of intimacy takes time.
8. Guarding your heart is always being prepared to run away from a relationship if God tells you to. You must see the signs that God gives you for this.

Recommendations for not getting romantically involved with the spouse candidate, and being prepared to flee at any time if necessary:

1. *Establish your prerequisites:* As I have mentioned in previous classes, the number one requirement for a marriage to work is that the person you are involved with is a good Christian.

2. *Focus on friendship:* control your mind so as not to indulge in fantasies. That is, do not daydream that he or she is already your husband or wife, this often ends up being something harmful where satan can gain the upper hand.

3. *Be firm with boundaries:* do not allow the guy to advance romantically in the relationship. This includes, as I have said, physical approach, but it also includes words and language that should be reserved only for marriage. Remember that if you marry that person, you will have plenty of time to enjoy those things, but for now (before marriage) you are only in the stage of knowledge and prayer, asking God to confirm that this man is the right one.

4. *Don't see him alone:* Don't be tempted to spend time alone with him. This means that you should see him only when other people are around (e.g. church activities). At a meal, for example, you can invite your brother or another trusted person to join you.

5. *Make your method and intentions clear from the beginning:* It is very important that you are honest. You do not need to lie, and you will not do so. Talk to your friend from the beginning about your intentions, and how you want the relationship to continue until the end. Be honest and tell him that at any time, you will be able to do it.

6. *Continue your development:* do not invest too much time in this relationship, nor allow it to become obsessive. Continue developing your growth in your spiritual life, in your studies and in your profession, etc.

7. *Keep a diary:* it is highly advisable that you keep a diary exclusively for this relationship and write down the most important events. Stay objective, so that you can later evaluate and not be carried away by feelings.

8. *Have a mentor:* it is highly advisable that you keep a mentor informed of what you are writing down in the diary. This mentor should preferably be your father/mother. If this is not possible, then it could be the pastors of the church or a mature Christian couple.

9. *Get involved in shared activities:* try to get to know the candidate in group activities, mostly at church or community activities, e.g. on missionary trips. In this way, you will get to know him in different situations.

Other Bible passages on the theme for reading and memorization

2 Ti. 2:22; 2 Cor. 6:14; 1 Cor. 13:4-7; 1 Cor. 15:33; Gn. 2:18; 1 Cor. 6:18; Gn. 2:24; Prov. 4:23; Heb. 13:4; Prov. 18:22; 1 Ts. 4:3-5; Rom. 12:9-140; Am. 3.3; Prov. 19:14.

85

Do Not Accept False Ideas

Memorize

Colossians 2:8 "See to it that no one takes you captive by philosophy and empty deceit, according to human tradition, according to the elemental spirits of the world, and not according to Christ."

You now live in the 21st century, an era of great technological advancement, but also a time when there are many ideas that are contrary to the Bible. You as a Christian, must not only reject those ideas, but also, you must preach the truth of the Scriptures, because God has called us to be light in the darkness.

? Introductory Questions

1. What are some ideas (from your teachers or classmates) that you have heard at school that you think are contrary to the Bible?
2. Why do you think you should express God's ideas to people?
3. How can you exercise your right to express your opinion and preach about Jesus?

Bible Story (Acts 7:1-60)

True Christians are peaceful people and stay away from conflicts as far as possible. We love everyone and do not discriminate against anyone. However, at the same time, we are brave in standing up against all the false ideas that are dragging humanity down. These ideas deceive people into believing that they are good, but they are destructive ideas. You, as a Christian, should not be afraid to express God's truth in private and in public, and to defend your faith.

Now I will mention some of these lying ideas that are popular today. You will see some words that you may not know, but it is good that you start to know and understand them. I will explain them to you in a simple way: 1) <u>Moral relativism</u>: there are no absolute truths, but everything depends on how each person sees it. For example, sex before marriage is neither good nor bad, but depends on how each person thinks; 2) <u>Evolution</u>: that man descends from the monkey; God is not the Creator, but everything was formed alone; 3) <u>Materialism</u>: miracles do not exist, nor spiritual things, everything is matter; 4) <u>Gender ideologies</u>: that there are more than two sexes (man and woman) and that everyone can have the sex they want; 5) <u>Humanism</u>: the human being is the center, not God, God is only a servant of the human being, an invention of the human being; 6) <u>Feminism</u>: men and women do not complement each other but are fighting for power.

If you <u>do not</u> agree with these ideas, I congratulate you, because true Christians will never agree with any of these ideas, but I will also tell you something: you could be persecuted. In the biblical passage, Stephen was stoned because he expressed the ideas of God and preached to others about Jesus. And you, are you willing to have some people not accept you for speaking about Jesus and His Word?

Illustration

The case of Kim Davis, in Kentucky, became known worldwide as a case of imprisonment for the defense of the traditional family. Kim Davis, a clerk in Rowan County, Kentucky, refused to issue marriage licenses to same-sex couples. Only a few days ago, the US federal government had legalized same-sex marriage in the Supreme Court in 2015; but Davis, being a good Christian, was brave and told them that her faith prevented her from validating such marriages.

Davis was sued and ended up in jail in September 2015. She spent five days there, and although she was thankfully released, her case shows that today a person could be persecuted for refusing to do what is <u>not</u> right before God. Christians obey the laws; however, we cannot do something contrary to God's commandments (Acts 4:19; 5:29). You must stand firm.

In 2016, due to Kentucky Governor Matt Bevin's initiative, officials are allowed an exception to the law if doing so conflicts with their religious beliefs. Thank God!

Questions About the Class

1. Why can't you, as a Christian, accept any idea that is contrary to the Bible?
2. Why should you fight ideas that are contrary to the Word of God?
3. Name three of the ideas that are contrary to the Bible mentioned in class with their short definition.
4. Why was Stephen stoned to death?
5. What would you have done if you had been in Kim Davis's place?
6. How did Kim Davis' courage change the law in the state of Kentucky?

Phrases to Memorize

1. Every true Christian is against ideas and philosophies contrary to the Bible.
2. Ideas contrary to the Bible are ideas that deceive human beings and lead them to condemnation, because God will not justify anyone's sin under the excuse that he was deceived.
3. Moral relativism, evolution, materialism, gender ideologies, humanism and feminism are examples of these destructive and anti-Christian ideas.
4. When you express that you do not agree with the above ideas you may suffer persecution, but do not worry, God will bless you for it and honor you.
5. You have the right to express your opinion and preach the truth to those who are now in darkness. They have the right to express themselves, just like you. Everyone has the right to hear the gospel: do not be silent.

Other Bible passages on the theme for reading and memorization

1 Pet. 3:15; 2 Ti. 4:1-22; Gal. 2:4-5; 2 Cor. 10:5; 1 Ti. 1:9; Jud. 1:3; 2 Ti. 2:24-25; Acts. 21:13; Mt. 5:11-12; 2 Ti. 2:3; 2 Ti. 2:8-9

Made in the USA
Monee, IL
19 August 2024